How to win more business
by phone, telex and fax

Bernard Katz

How to win more business by phone, telex and fax

Hutchinson Business

London Melbourne Auckland Johannesburg

Hutchinson Business
An imprint of Century Hutchinson Ltd
62–65 Chandos Place, London WC2N 4NW

Century Hutchinson Australia Pty Ltd
16–22 Church Street, Hawthorn, Melbourne, Victoria 3122

Century Hutchinson Group (NZ) Ltd
32–34 View Road, PO Box 40–086, Glenfield, Auckland 10

Century Hutchinson Group (SA) Pty Ltd
PO Box 337, Bergvlei 2012, South Africa

First published in 1983 under the title
How to Win More Business by phone
First published under present title in 1987

Set in 11 on 13 Palatino by
Input Typesetting Ltd, London SW19

Printed in Great Britain by
Mackays of Chatham Ltd

British Library Cataloguing in Publication data

Katz, Bernard, *1987*–
    How to win more business by phone, telex
    and fax.— 2nd ed.
    1. Telephone selling   2. Telecommunication
    I. Title   II. Katz, Bernard, *1987*– How
    to win more business by phone
    685.8'5   HF5438.3

ISBN 0–09–168000–X

Nessa Grindley —

London
April '87 –

To my children: Alexandra, Mark and Tim

Contents

Introduction

One of the most cost effective ways of winning more business is by phone. That was the premiss of my book when it was first published. It has not changed. Selling on the phone saves valuable time. But to make it work, the selling has to be efficient and professional.

Learning to sell on the phone is about learning how to use techniques. That is all. This book is packed with practical advice – how to make the first call, how to overcome feelings of apprehension and tension, what to do when the customer says 'no'. The planning and the structure of successful telephone selling are given, for managers who want to train others, and for sales people who want to learn for themselves and improve.

In this second edition the techniques are the same. There has been no need for change or 'updating'. Selling on the phone is successful if the techniques are used, in the way described.

New material, however, has been included which gives practical instruction for using telex and fax and high speed data transmission to get new business.

The working environment of business is changing. Technology has made communication much easier. Today, telex and fax are options in contacting buyers and decision makers that cannot be ignored. Telex messages have urgency. Fax has urgency. Messages sent in this way are seen with certainty. So there are additional, very powerful, marketing tools available in the search for new customers and contacts.

The phone, the prospecting letter, telex and fax have complementary uses in prospecting for business. In certain circumstances so does high speed data transmission. The reader is provided with advice, checklists and rules on how to use each – and when, for the greatest result. Throughout the book, a question and answer format is adopted, with a short list of 'test' questions at the beginning of each chapter. These questions are then worked through in the following pages, and the answers given. The reader's answers may differ from the ones given, but that does not necessarily mean they are wrong. The format has been adopted to act as a signpost to the different techniques and skills that win more business.

I make warm acknowledgements to Michael Gee, chief executive of Vitel International Ltd. for his expertise on high speed data transmission.

Training to improve performance in prospecting for business is carried out by many. I welcome contact, with criticism or suggestions. The solutions to training problems that are developed by dialogue, lead to new and useful teaching resources.

Bernard Katz
Telex: 295 441 BUSY B G
Fax: 209 1231

How to prospect for business by phone

In order to prospect successfully, a skill must be developed. The skill comes from applying a set of rules. The rules should apply to any business. This chapter develops a set of rules for prospecting by asking questions and using the answers.

Are the answers known already? Before reading this chapter, answer the test list of questions. Do this without reading the text first. The answers are worked through in the following pages and are summarized at the end of the chapter. The same test of knowledge is employed with each chapter.

Questions

1 When prospecting, who do we telephone?
2 Where do we find the names and addresses of prospective customers?
3 What interests the prospective customers most?
4 What are our objectives?
5 What is the best way of telephoning?
6 What records of prospecting calls must be kept?
7 When do we telephone the prospective customers?
8 How frequently should prospecting calls be made?
9 How is a better success rate achieved?

Answers

Chapter 1   How to prospect for business by phone

Selecting prospective customers – Locating prospective customers – What motivates customers? – What motivates us? – The best method of phoning – Keeping records – The best time of day – The right number of calls – Becoming more successful – Summary

Selecting prospective customers

Telephone prospecting is a skill. The questions that are asked about telephone prospecting search for a pattern of behaviour that brings success. The answers to the questions form the basis for a set of *Operating rules*. With practice, the *Operating rules* become easy to obey. The skill is then achieved.

Question: When prospecting, who do we telephone?
Answer: A carefully selected list of prospective customers.

We cannot telephone everybody in the telephone directory. Rather, we should not telephone every entry because some of the people that we would speak to could have no possible interest in our product or service. We must select prospective customers carefully.

Every business can divide its customers into a number of different customer categories. Each category has specific needs and requirements. For example, a sales representative for a motor distributor identifies the following major categories of car users:

1   Professional users – doctors, solicitors, architects, accountants.
2   Farmers.
3   Small businesses – shopkeepers, window cleaners, building contractors.
4   Hoteliers and restaurateurs.

5   Directors and executives of local industrial firms.

6   Transport managers of large organizations.

In this case, there are six categories, In another industry there may be five or seven, or perhaps three.

Each customer, within the different groups of customers, wants something different from a car to best satisfy his or her needs. The small businessman goes for a prestige model. The doctor wants low petrol consumption. For the farmer, durability is the most important factor. The same car, within the manufacturer's range, is well capable of satisfying the differing needs of different types of people. The car can do this because it has many distinct benefit features.

Restricting the prospecting calls to the major categories of customer that provide a business with its orders eliminates wasted calls. Wasted calls are those that have little or no chance of succeeding. A small chance is not enough. Every telephone prospecting call must have the full potential to be successful.

The first operating rule is now formulated. It establishes the method of eliminating the calls that are most certain to fail.

Operating rule 1

Identify the existing major categories of customer.

Select prospective customers from within these groupings.

Prepare a simple three column grid (the format is illustrated in Figure 1).

Enter the major customer categories in the first column.

Locating prospective customers

Question: Where do we find the names and addresses of prospective customers?

Answer: In specific publications, directories and records.

If the prospective customers are companies, their names and addresses are published in one or other of the directories available. (See Appendix for a list of useful sources.) Alternatively, the names of the companies will appear in a journal, newspaper or register. If

PROSPECTIVE CUSTOMER CATEGORIES	WHERE FOUND	PROSPECTIVE CUSTOMER NEEDS
1 Professional users	Year books *Yellow Pages* Professional journals	Status Comfort Economy Security
2 Farmers	Trade press *Yellow Pages* Local papers	Carrying capacity Ruggedness Versatility
3 Small businesses	Chamber of Commerce *Yellow Pages* Local press Trade press Trade directory	Carrying capacity Economy Reliability Status
4 Hoteliers and restaurateurs	Trade press *Yellow Pages* Trade directory	Carrying capacity Status Economy Reliability
5 Directors and executives of local industrial firms	*Kompass* *Yellow Pages* Trade publications	Status Comfort Reliability
6 Transport managers of large organizations	Trade press Local press *Yellow Pages*	Economy Reliability Security Carrying capacity

Figure 1 *The prospective customer grid*
As an illustration, the entries represent the major customer groupings of a motor car dealership located in a town where there are farming activities as well as light industry.

16

a company is anonymous, to the extent that its name cannot be found in published form, it is unlikely that it qualifies as a potential customer. Most businesses advertise themselves, if only by a line entry in a directory.

The directory giving the most detailed information is *Kompass*. It segments its data against many parameters – product type, distribution channels, turnover, resources employed, geographical location, etc. *Yellow Pages*, the most readily available directory, is helpful. However, the information it provides is restricted to a general company classification only. Callers can find lists of companies in any particular industry or trade, but no individual details are given.

Many businesses are lax about keeping a library of current directories, and those that are available are frequently years out of date. If telephone prospecting is to be successful, it is essential to keep an up to date library of relevant business directories. There is an alternative. The necessary information is available from the local public library reference section, or from a Chamber of Commerce library and librarians are usually helpful in guiding a researcher. One hour a week spent in a library provides names and telephone numbers for perhaps a week's telephone prospecting, or even longer.

If the prospective customers are private persons, electoral rolls supply names and addresses. The total number of persons living at an address is recorded and thus an indication of the size of a family in a dwelling is obtainable. No information other than bare demographic facts is given. Other information about private persons must be taken from announcements and classified advertisements in the national and local press.

Operating rule 2
Identify sources of names and addresses of prospective customers, falling within the major customer classifications.

Enter the reference sources in the middle column of the prospecting grid (see Figure 1).

What motivates customers?

Question: What interests the prospective customers most?
Answer: Anything that satisfies a customer's needs and wants should interest that customer.

To understand what interests prospective customers, in order to benefit from that knowledge, it is necessary to identify their *needs* and *wants*. These will vary within each customer grouping.

Needs are essential requirements. They must be fulfilled for the prospective customer to go about his or her daily business in the most satisfactory way. Consider an everyday item – shoes. In the case of an encyclopaedia sales representative, shoes are a necessity for fulfilling daily tasks. The prime *needs* of a person who does a lot of walking, such as a sales representative, might be classified as:
1   Comfort.
2   Durability.
The sales representative may also *want* the shoes to be:
1   Elegant.
2   Fashionable.
For example, he or she may want to wear crocodile leather shoes. He or she may want others to see that the shoes are expensive. This *want* is a desire. It is something that the salesperson would like to have. The *want*, however, is not a real *need*.

The *needs* and *wants* of a fashion model, as far as shoes are concerned, are very different. Her needs are that the shoes are:
1   Elegant.
2   Fashionable.
Her *wants* are that the shoes are comfortable. It is unlikely that durability is a feature, either as a *need* or a *want*.

Analysis of the buying process shows that a prospective customer makes a decision to purchase when:
1   Some or all of his or her *needs* are satisfied.
2   Some or all of his or her *wants* are satisfied.

A customer sometimes buys, acting on impulse, when the *wants* only are satisfied. The customer is much more likely to buy when the *needs* are met. Satisfaction of *needs* is provided by means of *benefit messages*. These are passed by the sales representative to the customer. Sometimes the customer perceives them spontaneously.

There is no set formula for passing benefit messages. They can be verbal or visual and can also be perceived by touch, sound, taste or smell. Benefit messages are frequently direct and to the point. For example, the shoe salesperson says:

'These shoes are very comfortable and strong. They will last you a very long time.'

In making these statements, the shoe salesperson is satisfying the *needs* of comfort and durability. The statement would not, however, be effective in generating a buying decision from the fashion model. It does not relate to her *needs*.

In the case of the motor car distributor, six major prospective customer categories were identified (these are entered in the prospect grid of Figure 1). The following needs are identified for the different categories:

Professional users	status comfort economy security
Farmers	carrying capacity ruggedness versatility
Small businesses	carrying capacity economy reliability status
Hoteliers and restaurateurs	carrying capacity status economy reliability
Directors and executives of local industrial firms	status comfort reliability
Transport managers of large organizations	economy reliability security carrying capacity

The above *needs* have been identified by sales representatives in the

19

motor trade employed by a particular dealership. Other representatives do not necessarily make identical judgements. Experience in the particular industry, in the particular locality and within a particular work environment all contribute to the representative's judgement of the *needs* of a specific customer category. There is nothing to prevent *needs* being common to different user classes. Hence a particular model of motor car is the right model for prospective customers in different occupations and having differing life styles. The important thing is that the *needs* that a prospective customer does have are identified.

Operating rule 3
Identify the major needs of the different prospective customer categories.
Enter the needs in column 3 of the prospecting grid (see Figure 1).

What motivates us?

Question: What are our objectives?
Answer: Our objectives vary in relation to the product or service to be sold. They are:
1   Achieving a sale.
2   Arranging a demonstration appointment.

Situation 1

The salesperson working for a trade journal or selling advertising space in a publication expects to secure a firm order when a prospective customer is telephoned. The sequence of the cold prospecting call is as follows:

1   The prospective customer is dialled.
2   Contact is made.
3   Caller introduces himself or herself.
4   Caller qualifies the prospective customer – to make sure that time is not wasted selling to a person without the authority to buy.

5   Benefit messages are passed to satisfy the needs the prospective customer is known to have – or assessed to have.
6   An offer is made.
7   Customer objections are countered.
8   The order is closed.

Sometimes the call is more complicated. Trial closes are made and fresh objections are uncovered and countered. Success is never automatic. None the less, when a sale is achieved it is through the medium of a cold prospecting telephone call.

Situation 2

With some products or services success in a prospecting call is never achieved – no matter how brilliant and experienced the salesperson is. A car, a house, a diamond or life assurance can never be sold within the space of one cold prospecting call. This does not mean that companies selling cars or houses should never prospect. It means, simply, that they have different objectives.

Objectives are different depending on the nature and the price of the product or service. When it is not possible to secure an order as a result of a prospecting call, it is because insufficient information can be supplied to the buyer during the conversation. The level of communication is inadequate because conversation by itself is not sufficient. The prospective customer has to be in a situation where the benefit messages received from the salesperson are reinforced by seeing, touching, hearing or tasting the product.

Situation 3

The objective is to arrange for an opportunity to provide the prospective customer with the necessary total information.

When a prospecting call fails, whatever the objective, it does not necessarily mean that a sale is never going to be achieved. It means that in the short duration of the call, the salesperson has failed on one or more different levels.

Reasons for failure

1   The prospective customer is not correctly 'qualified' as to whether he or she makes the decision to purchase.

Example A hardware manufacturer telephones a department store hoping to open an account. Contact is made with the hardware department. The telephone is answered by the manager, who is receptive to the prospecting call. At the end of the conversation no purchase is possible, or appointment made because all buying is carried out centrally from a distant head office.

2 The *needs* of the prospective customer are not analysed correctly.

Example A forwarding agent telephones a prospective exporter customer. It is established that a substantial amount of business is carried out with Dutch and German markets. The prospecting caller emphasizes the very competitive roll-on roll-off container service available. No order is obtained because, whilst some overland business is undertaken by the exporter, the prime physical distribution *needs* are for faster air-freight. The caller has established some *needs*, but not the principal ones.

3 The prospective customer's objections are not overcome.

Example The prospective customer says 'I will think about it'. At that point the caller retires from the conversation. Instead, the caller should probe into what precisely is going to be thought about.

4 Insufficient information about the product is provided.

5 The objective is to gain an appointment to present the product. The caller tries to sell the product details instead of the product concept.

Example A manufacturer of vibrating pads, designed to relieve pain and tension, telephones a prospective customer at home. The caller stresses price and minimal after sales service requirements. No order is given. Instead, the caller should have stressed relief from pain.

Some reasons for failure lie with the prospective customer:

1 Insufficient information regarding the prospective customer's own resources is available to allow a decision to be made.

Example Producers of management training films telephone a business college. Contact is made with the departmental head who has authority to purchase supplies. However, until the departmental head is certain that the films can be shown on the college video equipment, no purchasing decision is possible.

2   Insufficient time is given for the offer to be considered.

3   The customer has inadequate resources.

The second chance

If the primary objective of a prospecting call – whether it is a sale or an appointment – cannot be achieved, a secondary objective is the chance to have another go. The secondary objective is achieved by the technique of 'leaving the door open'. The sequence is as follows:

1   Prospecting call to point where no further progress is possible.
2   Statement that literature or samples are being sent for the buyer to consider.
3   Statement that the caller will telephone in about five days' time to answer any queries that arise.
4   Immediate close of the conversation.

Under no circumstances is permission asked to send the literature and under no circumstances is the prospective customer asked if the caller might telephone in a few days' time. A direct question invites a categorical 'No' especially when the early part of the conversation has not been successful.

Example
   Buyer   '. . . so I must repeat, Mr Caller, we are well serviced by our suppliers. I have no need for an additional manufacturer at the present time.'
   Caller   'I understand, Mr Buyer. I tell you what I will do. I will put all the literature regarding our product range into the post to you. I will telephone in about five days' time, to answer any queries that may arise. Goodbye, Mr Buyer.'

The caller is firm and positive and states what is going to happen. This way, the prospective customer knows that contact is going to be made again. More than likely the caller is dismissed from mind the moment that the receiver is put down. But when the second call is made the name is remembered.

Operating rule 4
Identify the primary and secondary objectives that must be achieved.

The best method of phoning

Question: What is the best way of telephoning?
Answer: Prospecting calls must always follow a prepared script.

Prospecting calls must always be made from a prepared script. The conversation should follow a strict plan, though the prospective customer does not know that there is a plan. It is, however, prepared in advance to cover all the different types of answers and objections that could be offered.

The use of the script gives complete control of the conversation. It also gives confidence to the caller and usually leads to the primary or secondary objectives being achieved.

Actually speaking on the telephone is the culmination of all the preparation. It is the moment of truth that follows the learning and

practising of the operating rules. The speaking part of telephone prospecting is so important that it warrants another set of rules. They are so basic and necessary that they are called the *Golden rules*.

Every successful call makes use of the *Golden rules*. The *Golden rules* influence and direct the structure of the telephone prospecting script.

Golden rule 1
Always smile when speaking to the prospective customer.

Smiling is consciously relaxing. A friendly courteous manner communicates itself to the other end of the telephone.

Golden rule 2
Involve the prospective customer in conversation as early as possible.

At all costs the prospective customer must not be talked *at*. If the telephone has to be held at arm's length to avoid the torrent of words pouring out, the objective will never be reached.

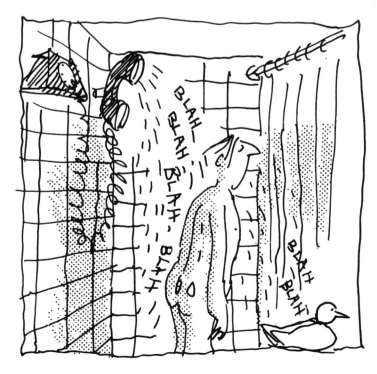

25

Golden rule 3
Ask frequent questions.

The prospective customer must be 'qualified' by the caller to find out the following information:

Needs: What the customer must have.

Wants: What the customer would like to have.

Time scale: When the customer will be ready to buy.

Money: Ability to pay.

If the prime objective is not a sale, but a demonstration appointment, special care must be taken. There is little value in securing an appointment if the prospective customer realistically cannot afford to buy. This situation does not arise when the objective is a straight sale. No customer without money makes a commitment for an immediate purchase.

An experienced salesperson may well manage to secure a demonstration appointment but if it does not lead to a sale it is a waste of time. All demonstration appointments must subsequently be converted into sales. Wasted appointments can be minimized by correct qualification of the prospective customer in the first place. This is most effectively achieved by asking pertinent questions.

Golden rule 4
The prospective customer listens only as long as he or she is interested.

A prospective customer does not necessarily want views on the weather, or on the performance of the local football team. He or she may not want to listen as the caller's company is described in minute detail. But, most people are courteous. Because a prospective customer is courteous the caller is not told abruptly to go away. Licence to ramble on does not, however, guarantee an order. Only the full attention of the prospective customer to what is being said allows the caller's objective to be attained. A customer pays full attention when his or her wants or needs are being discussed. The caller's product or service may be the best in the world but if it does not satisfy the prospective customer's needs or wants it will not be of interest.

Golden rule 5
Always aim at achieving the objectives.

A pleasant, easy conversation, by itself, does not secure a sale. There must be control at all times, moving in a planned way towards the objectives.

On the telephone, not a second must be wasted. Every word and every question must contribute to reaching the desired goal.

Golden rule 6
When the prospective customer says 'No', selling must start.

'No' is an objection that must be overcome. The drive towards achieving the objective is then continued. The 'No' might take the form of:

Not now. . . . .
Next time we buy. . . .
Too much stock. . . .
Business is bad. . . .
No money. . . .

The objections might be a smoke screen. They might be product criticism. There might be misinterpretation of information. The prospective customer's 'No' is not a signal for the caller to say 'Thank you for listening' and to put the telephone down. It is a signal that efforts must be redoubled to identify the real needs of the customer – and to supply appropriate benefits to meet those needs.

Writing the script

The telephone script is the plan that leads the caller through to achieving the objectives. The script incorporates the *Golden rules*. The structure of the script is as follows:

1   Contact is established with the correct person.
2   A reason for calling is provided.
3   The prospective customer is qualified, to ensure that there is value in proceeding.
4   Benefit messages are given to meet the needs of the customer.
5   A trial close is made.
6   If unsuccessful, customer objections are identified and countered.
7   Additional benefit messages are given.
8   Close for prime objective.
9   If unsuccessful, close for second objective.

The body of the telephone prospecting script is built onto the basic structure in the form of an algorithm – a verbal flow chart that is constructed to deal with every response that the caller receives.

Illustration: The script used by Hayden Manor Consultants Ltd to prospect for business.

Scenario: Hayden Manor Consultants Ltd are a firm of management consultants. The major business activities are providing training systems to industry and commerce. To obtain business, Hayden Manor Consultants Ltd must find companies who have problems. They solve these problems by developing and leading training programmes for the company. The training courses give new skills, or corrected skills, to the client company personnel.

Hayden Manor Consultants Ltd are specialists. In many cases they work with companies who already have their own training division. These divisions are usually headed by a training manager, but he or she will not have the specialist expertise of Hayden Manor Consultants Ltd.

The consultants obtain new business in three ways:

1   Recommendations from satisfied clients.
2   Advertising.
3   PROSPECTING.

The nature of the script as a flow chart is immediately shown by the opening sequence:

Caller   'Hello. May I speak to the training manager, please?'
Customer   'Certainly. Would you tell me who is calling?'

This approach gets through. It does not, however, reveal the name of the training manager. A better initial approach is:

Caller   'Hello. I want to speak to the training manager please, but before you put me through, would you tell me the person's name?'
Customer   'Mr Brown.'
Caller   'Oh thank you. Would you put me through now please?'

The reply here is straightforward. It may not be. The first problem is often met at this stage. Instead, the caller is asked:

'Can you tell me what it is about?'

Never go into detail until talking to the right person:

'Oh yes. Company training. What is the name of the training manager?'

The answer is short, and in general terms. An authoritative tone of voice discourages further questions.

A further problem arises from time to time. Not every tele-phonist is perfect. Sometimes the telephonist begins to put the call through before the caller has even finished speaking. At other times one is left holding on and on. Alternatively, the caller is connected to someone who is not even remotely concerned with the matter of the call. The next statement, therefore, if there is any doubt at all, is:

'Good morning, Mr Brown. Am I talking to the training manager?'

Already, *Golden rule 2* is employed. (It is assumed that the caller is smiling and that *Golden rule 1* is in force.) *Golden rule 3* is being used too.

If the reply is 'No':

'Oh. I have been wrongly connected. I am sorry for this trouble. Would you kindly put me through to the training manager?'

If the reply is 'Yes' the call proceeds:

Caller 'We are the Hayden Manor Consultants Ltd and my name is John Brentwood. Do you know us?'
Customer 'I am sorry Mr Brentwood. I am afraid that I do not appear to know you.'
Caller 'Oh, I am sorry to hear that. Hayden Manor is in fact a magnificent English country mansion, over one thousand years old. More importantly, we provide tailor made training courses for industry in most of the major disciplines: finance, marketing, salesmanship, personnel management, computer skills. Do you have any training needs at the present time?'

A reason for calling is given. Questions are asked. The prospective customer is drawn into the conversation. 'Do you know us?' is a flexible question. Whether the customer answers *'Yes'* or *'No'*, the same message is given:

Customer 'Yes. I think that I have heard of your company.'
Caller 'Oh good. You may know then that Hayden Manor itself is a magnificent country mansion. More importantly, you will know that we provide tailor made training courses for industry. We cover most of the major disciplines . . .'

The customer is then asked to qualify his or her needs with a direct question:

'Do you have any training needs at the present time?'

If the answer is positive:

> *Customer* 'Well, we have continuing training needs of one kind or another.'
>
> *Caller* 'Good. We would like an opportunity of talking to you, to see if we can offer training systems that might be of interest. Why don't you have lunch with us one day next week at the Manor? You could pop into one or two of the seminar rooms to see us in action. We could talk about any of the specific problems you may have. Would next Tuesday or Thursday be more convenient?'

An offer is given. The conversation moves straight towards the prime objective. This follows on from a positive response to the qualifying question. If the reply is negative, more benefit messages are necessary.

> *Caller* 'Do you have any training needs at the present time?'
>
> *Customer* 'No, not really. We have not formulated any plans for training at the present time, other than product knowledge. That is covered adequately. Thank you for contacting us, but no.'

Acting on *Golden rule 6*, the caller does not give up, but continues:

> *Caller* 'Mr Brown, I would like to tell you that most of our clients in the private sector said, at the outset, that they had not yet decided what was the best course of action for them to take. As an example, this was the situation with Shell, with the Metal Box Company, with Bowater Scott. We talked with them, generally, about business. You know, they are all very large companies. We identified areas that they considered were not as efficient as they might have been. In every case we went away and thought about the problem. When we went back we made suggestions as to how improvements could be achieved by training their personnel. In each case we were subsequently invited to train and each time it was extremely successful. We are now acting for each company in a number of different fields. By the way, how do you sell your merchandise? Is it through a national distributor network?'
>
> *Customer* 'Yes.'

Caller 'Are you satisfied that the sales operation is as effective as it might be?'

Customer 'Well no. There is always room for improvement.'

Caller 'We have a lot of experience in this field, Mr Brown. Why don't you have lunch with us one day next week, at the Manor? You could see us in action and we could talk about any of the specific problems that you may have. Would next Tuesday or Thursday be more convenient?'

Customer 'I am sure that your company could help us Mr Brentwood, but I am afraid that at the present time I am too busy to consider the matter.'

Caller 'I see, Mr Brown. Well, I tell you what I will do. I will put some literature into the post about our activities. I never send literature cold. I imagine that, like others, you are bombarded with literature. Is that so?'

Customer 'Yes. It is quite true.'

Caller 'Good. I will telephone you, Mr Brown, in about six days time to make sure that the literature has arrived and to answer any queries that arise. Goodbye, Mr Brown.'

When it becomes clear that the prime objective cannot be achieved, the conversation is directed towards the second objective.

Figure 2 shows the conversation script in diagrammatic form. Each part of the conversation is a bloc leading to a further bloc, depending on the reply of the customer.

Operating rule 5
Write the script for the prospecting call.
Structure the script to incorporate both 'Yes' and 'No' answers (see Figure 2).
Follow the Golden rules at all times.

Keeping records

Question What records of prospecting calls must be kept?
Answer: Important details in brief of each call on a simple card index system.

Keeping a record of all calls made is almost as important as the

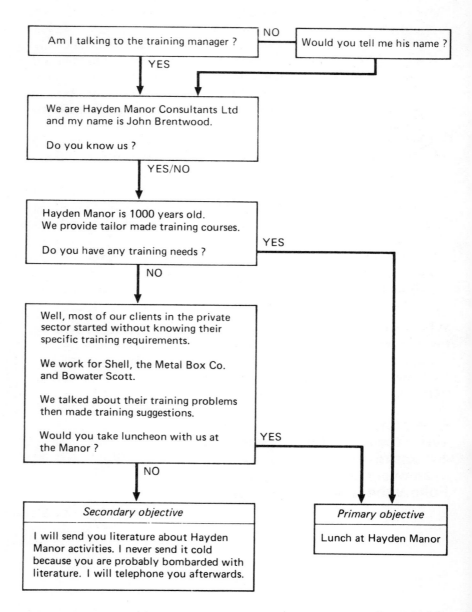

Figure 2 *Example of prospecting script showing individual 'blocs' within the conversation and the alternative response directions*

prospecting call itself. Prospecting is extremely effective in securing orders but that does not mean to say the administration has to be complicated. The records that need to be kept are simple. An index card is all that is required. The card is divided into five columns (see Figure 3). In the first column the name of the contact is entered and in the second column, the company name. The telephone number goes into the third column, and in the fourth, the company's address. Column five is for comments and ACTION.

Every prospective customer lead is valuable. If a prospective customer is called and he or she is not in, the call must be made again later. If the caller does not bother, but just moves on to the next name and telephone number, sooner or later the available leads will dry up. It is tempting, and easy, just to move on. It is also much less bother to leave out the names and addresses and the ACTION details. The temptation is to think that every detail is going to be remembered. Memory, however, is unreliable. Every relevant detail must be recorded, even though it is tedious. If a

Contact name	Company name	Telephone number	Prospect address	ACTION

Figure 3   *Format of index card for keeping records of prospecting calls*

message is given to the caller that the prospective customer is out, but will be in his or her office mid-afternoon on Tuesday, then that is the time when a second call must be made. Whatever instructions are given to the caller, they must be entered for ACTION accordingly.

Every day the index cards should be looked through to see which call-backs must be made. When it is decided that a prospective customer is no longer worth expending effort over, and when it is certain that no further benefit is available from additional contact, the name of the company should be scored out by drawing a line through the entry. It should not be erased or blocked out completely as, some time later, when the lists are checked, it will be necessary to know which companies have already been contacted. Even the best memories do not always remember every single detail.

The information on the index card must be filled in before each call, except for the ACTION column. This is completed immediately afterwards. It is unwise to leave the records until the end of the day. When there is a delay, entries are often overlooked.

Operating rule 6
Prepare and maintain a simple records system for all prospecting calls made.
Record name of contact, telephone number, name of company, address and ACTION result of initial call. Record also if a sale is achieved, if it is necessary to make contact again, or if there is no further value in a second call.

The best time of day

Question: When do we telephone the prospective customers?
Answer: The times are variable depending on the business habits of the different customer groups. As a general rule, calls are made in the afternoon, when telephone charges are cheaper.

At the time of going to press it is considerably more costly to telephone in the morning up to 1.00 p.m. A realistic costing of cold canvass expenses compared with the cost of local telephone prospecting calls made in the morning would still show the telephone prospecting method to be more cost effective. If, however, customers live some distance away, telephone calls may need to be restricted to the afternoon.

There is no set time, applicable to all prospective customers, when it is most effective to telephone. A caller soon establishes that there is a pattern relating to each different customer category. For example, a builder is in his office at 7.30 a.m. – before the expensive call period commences. A doctor is available to receive calls at the end of morning surgery. This is at about 11.30 a.m. and falls into the expensive rate bracket. The call should be made instead before afternoon surgery commences, at about 4.30 p.m.

Telephone prospecting is an activity that must also fit into the caller's own business timetable. There are free minutes during the day – in between meetings, before interviews, after a tea break. Whatever the occupation or profession of the caller, short intervals can be found in his or her day and they are all opportunities for a prospective customer to be telephoned. The times when calls can be made during the day are totally flexible. The situation alters only when a customer indicates that he or she is to be called back at a certain time. In this case there is no flexibility. If the ACTION column of the record card says '11.00 a.m. on Monday 24th Mr Grimes is in his office', then that is the time, without fail, at which Mr Grimes must be telephoned, irrespective of other commitments.

Operating rule 7
Whenever possible, telephone in the afternoon when calls are cheaper.
Establish by trial and error the best times of day for telephoning different customer categories.
When a call back time is specified in the ACTION column of the record card, always telephone punctually.

The right number of calls

Question: How frequently should prospecting calls be made?
Answer: The number of calls is decided in the context of the caller's work programme.

The decision as to the number of calls to be made per day, is one that is made in the context of the work programme. A prospecting target is planned in advance. Prospecting is not successful if the target decision, made each morning, is dependent on whether it is raining or whether there are only a few appointments or meetings on a given day. The target number, whatever it is, must be kept to. It must be remembered that, out of all the calls, a number are converted into sales or into demonstration appointments and these require administration time. There is another factor as well. There must be telephone numbers of prospective customers to ring and getting these numbers takes time. If the *Yellow Pages* are being used, the amount of time required is small. Going to a library takes longer and making special journeys to buy a newspaper or trade journal also takes up time. Everything that contributes to delay must be taken into account when planning the target number of prospecting calls in order for the target to be realistic.

When telephone prospecting is first started as a new activity, it is valuable to set a trial period – two weeks is a useful length of time. A realistic target number of calls for this period is then worked out. On a blank index card draw the target record grid illustrated in Figure 4. Enter the dates of the initial two week trial period in the first two columns. Then enter the target number of calls to be made and the caller's judgement of how many times the primary objectives will be achieved.

	Dates		Number to be made		Number of objectives achieved	
	from:	to:	Cold telephone calls	Prospecting letters	from telephone calls	from prospecting letters
Target						
Actual						
Target						
Actual						
Target						
Actual						

Figure 4   *Target record grid*

The other columns in the grid relate to prospecting by letter. The subject of prospecting letters is dealt with later but in many cases a programme of prospecting letters goes hand in hand with prospecting telephone calls. It is necessary to monitor the success performance in both prospecting activities carefully.

Operating rule 8
Decide on a target number of prospecting calls for a two week trial period.
Draw a target record grid and enter target number of calls and objectives set against actual number of calls and achievement (see Figure 4).

Becoming more successful

Question: How is a better success rate achieved?
Answer: Monitoring prospecting calls, thus identifying strengths and weaknesses, leads to improved performance.

If one primary objective is achieved from every four calls, is this a successful rate? Is a success rate of one in eight or one in twelve still acceptable? Success is measured by cost effectiveness and this varies with different industries. Within each frame of reference, the strengths and weaknesses of the prospecting call should be measured.

Telephone prospecting works! If the calls do not get results, then something is wrong. The calls must be monitored to identify where the fault lies. A Do-It-Yourself checklist of faults is shown in Figure 5.

A reliable method of monitoring a prospecting call is to record it on a tape recorder. Inexpensive microphones with a small attachment that connects onto the telephone mouthpiece can be bought at most reputable audio equipment shops. Alternatively, there is more expensive equipment available that cradles the entire telephone, leaving both hands free.

The recorded call is then carefully analysed using the analysis grid, as shown in Figure 6, to find out the extent to which the *Golden rules* have been incorporated.

CHECKLIST	Yes	No
Is the prospective customer brought into the conversation early enough ?	☐	☐
Is the main customer *need* identified?	☐	☐
Are the objections identified ?	☐	☐
Are correct benefit messages given in relation to the customer's needs ?	☐	☐
Is the close effective ?	☐	☐
Is the script amended after analysis of unsatisfactory calls ?	☐	☐
Is the call allowed to deviate from the script ?	☐	☐
Are the prospective customer categories realistic ?	☐	☐
Are the calls made at the wrong time of the day ?	☐	☐
Have the *Golden rules* been followed ?	☐	☐
Are the follow-up ACTION requirements scrupulously observed ?	☐	☐
Is the call given up when the prospective customer says 'No' ?	☐	☐

Figure 5   *A checklist of faults*

Early prospective customer involvement			Frequent questions asked			Attainment of objectives				Interest sustained		Termination of call			Objections handled		Benefit messages	
Correct	Too early	Late	Correct	Too many	Too few	Sale demos		Literature		Yes	No	Correct	Early	Late	Well	Badly	Correct	Incorrect/ insufficient
						Yes	No	Yes	No									

Figure 6 *Telephone prospecting analysis grid*

Column 1   How quickly is the prospective customer involved in the call? Is it too early, too late, or just right?

Column 2   Are sufficient questions asked? Questions at the beginning of the conversation are particularly effective as they bring the customer into the conversation. Questions also identify the customer's *needs*.

Column 3   Was the call successful? Which objectives are obtained?

Column 4   Was the customer's interest sustained throughout or were the customer's replies merely courtesy?

Column 5   Was the call terminated at the right time? Sales can be lost by continuing a conversation. Once an objective is achieved the call must be closed politely and firmly.

Column 6   How well are the objections handled? Is this area the stumbling block to increased success?

Column 7   Benefit messages must be right for the customer's particular needs. Are the benefits right and are they sufficient?

Analysing the recorded telephone calls and making relevant entries in the columns of an analysis grid provides the caller with a profile of the prospecting calls. The areas of weakness can be seen and corrections are then made to the prospecting script. Analysis of subsequent recorded calls shows whether earlier mistakes are rectified.

Operating rule 9
Monitor telephone prospecting call performance by first recording the calls on a tape recorder.
Play the calls back and identify areas of weakness using the telephone prospecting analysis grid (see Figure 6).

Summary

Questions	Answers
1 When prospecting, who do we telephone?	A carefully selected list of prospective customers.
2 Where do we find the names and addresses of prospective customers?	In specific publications, directories and records.
3 What interests the prospective customers most?	Anything that satisfies a customer's needs and wants.
4 What are our objectives?	Our objectives vary in relation to the product or service to be sold. They are either achieving a sale or arranging a demonstration appointment.
5 What is the best way of telephoning?	Prospecting calls must always follow a prepared script.
6 What records of prospecting calls must be kept?	Important details in brief of each call on a simple card index system.
7 When do we telephone the prospective customers?	The times are variable depending on the business habits of the different customer groups. As a general rule, calls are made in the afternoon, when telephone charges are cheaper.
8 How frequently should prospecting calls be made?	The number of calls is decided in the context of the caller's work programme.
9 How is a better success rate achieved?	Monitoring prospecting calls, thus identifying strengths and weaknesses, leads to improved performance.

Chapter 2

How to get appointments

Before reading this chapter answer the following questions to test how much you know about getting appointments. Give your answers quickly. Do not think for a long time. The questions are repeated at the end of the chapter, together with the answers.

Questions

Answers

1 When trying to make an appointment who does one ask to speak to?

2 When put through to the buyer, what is said to confirm that it is the buyer speaking?

3 What questions find out if the buyer is interested?

4 What is the best way to deal with gate-keepers?

5 What is the best way of getting past secretaries?

6 What should be done when the buyer is out?

7 What is the best way of introducing oneself?

8 What is the best way to start the conversation with the buyer?

9 What should be done when the buyer says 'No' to an appointment?

10 Should one always write to the buyer before telephoning?

Chapter 2   How to get appointments

The person to contact – Making sure it's the right person – Is the buyer likely to be interested? – What to do about gate-keepers – The secretary hurdle – The absent buyer – The right form of greeting – Useful opening gambits – Dealing with refusal – Paving the way by letter – Summary

The person to contact

Question: When trying to make an appointment who does one ask to speak to?

Answer: One asks to speak to the buyer by name or by buying function.

When a company is small, the function of buyer is usually carried out by the owner or by one of the directors. As companies grow in size, a buyer, or a number of buyers, are appointed to specialist purchasing roles. Sometimes a company sets aside specific days and times when a buyer will see anyone who calls. In other companies the buyer makes his or her appointments when the need to buy arises.

When telephoning a prospective customer, the caller does not usually know the company policy. The problem is overcome by asking questions which are direct and to the point:

'What is the name of the buyer for haberdashery?'
'Is there a specific buyer for automotive equipment spares?'
'Is there a specified time when the flour buyer sees callers?'

Making sure it's the right person

Question: When put through to the buyer, what is said to confirm that it is the buyer speaking?

Answer: A direct question of confirmation is asked, so that the prospecting call may proceed.

When a person has a skill, little conscious thought is given to the individual sequence of actions that make up that skill. Walking is a skill, but nobody, when stepping off the pavement to cross the road, thinks of the complicated sequence of body weight changes and movements taking place. Instead, the person concentrates on avoiding any cars or other pedestrians on the road. In the skill of telephone prospecting, the process of making sure that one is correctly put through to a designated person may be compared with the body weight changes and movements in stepping off the pavement. It is something that must be done quickly and smoothly as a reflex action.

The caller makes sure that a Mr Hawkins really is Mr Hawkins or that the hosiery buyer really is the hosiery buyer. The process is very quick and straightforward. Direct questions are asked:

'Am I speaking to Mr Hawkins?'
'My name is John Edwards. Am I speaking to the hosiery buyer?'
'I asked to speak to the hosiery buyer. Am I speaking to the right person?'

Is the buyer likely to be interested?

Question: What questions find out if the buyer is interested?

Answer: There are five questions that the caller uses, each of which is designed to elicit a specific reply. The appropriate questions to use are planned in advance.

The neutral closed question

This invites a 'Yes' or 'No' answer. It elicits a specific short factual reply:

'Do you speak Italian?'
'Have you been to the Motor Show yet?'
'Is there union representation in your work force?'

The neutral closed question is normally used as part of a battery of questions. It does not, by itself, invite an elaborate reply but it is useful in identifying or eliminating subject areas so that further questions may follow:

Caller   'Do you export to America?'
Buyer   'No.'
Caller   'Would you be interested in selling your goods there?'
Buyer   'Yes.'
Caller   'We can . . .'

Neutral closed questions usually begin with:

'Would you . . .?'
'Do you . . .?'
'Can you . . .?'

The neutral open question

The objective of the neutral open question is to obtain a lot of information. The form of reply is deliberately not structured by the questioner. No matter how comprehensive the answer, the information given is only as much as the person wants to give.

Examples

'What are the factors that will influence your decision?'
'How does the production manager decide that the strengths of the catalysing agents are adequate?'
'Why was the sub-committee meeting postponed?'

The neutral leading question

The scene is set and limits are therefore imposed on the answer that is given. The person to whom the question is asked has the freedom to make any reply, but a reply that has specific reference to a particular subject area. Usually neutral leading questions start with 'When . . .?', 'Who . . .?' or 'Where . . .?'.

Examples

'When did you find that the parts were faulty?'
'Who was responsible for the strike?'
'Where will I find duplicate copies?'

The loaded minus question

The questioner strongly influences the reply in a negative context. The loaded minus question starts with:

'You wouldn't . . .'
'You don't . . .'
'You haven't . . .'

The person asking the question also shakes his or her head while speaking, so that the person being questioned is led, very strongly, to produce a negative answer. When using the loaded minus question the head is shaken even when speaking on the telephone. The principle involved is that of *Golden rule* 1 – always smile when speaking to the prospective customer. Body signals reinforce the spoken word.

Examples

'You don't think, in the circumstances, that we ought to continue supplying them, do you?'
'You haven't decided to resist the chairman's wishes, have you?'

The loaded plus question

Like the neutral leading question, the loaded plus question guides the answer that is obtained. The questioner puts his or her question in a framework of compliment and respect. An effort and a strong will are needed by the person replying in order to move away from the direction that has been pre-set.

Examples

'Mr Councillor, you have had years of experience of making this type of arrangement. You do agree that it is the best sequence of events, don't you?'

'Mr Smith, You are by far the most photogenic in the group. You do agree that you should be the one to face the television cameras, don't you?'

Making the effort to learn and adopt these questioning techniques is rewarding. Use of the techniques moves a telephone conversation quickly along a structured path. This is illustrated by the different prospecting conversations that a knitwear manufacturer, Cable Stitch Knitwear Co. Ltd, has with prospective customers:

Telephonist 'You are through now to Mr Patel.'
Caller 'Hello, Mr Patel. My name is Robert Riley of Cable Stitch Knitwear Co. Ltd. Do you buy knitwear?'
Buyer 'Yes.'
Caller 'Do you buy men's knitwear?'
Buyer 'Yes, we do.'
Caller 'Do you buy heavyweight knitwear for external wear and sportswear?'
Buyer 'Yes. We have some in stock now. . . .'

Here three neutral closed questions were used. However, one neutral open question would have produced the same information, more quickly and efficiently.

Telephonist 'You are through now to Mr Patel.'
Caller 'Hello, Mr Patel. My name is Robert Riley of Cable Stitch Knitwear Co. Ltd. What kind of knitwear do you buy?'

Before making the prospecting call, the right questions to use should be planned in advance. The following short checklist will help with planning.

Checklist

What is the information required?
What are the questions that will get the information quickly?

What are the best neutral open questions to use?

Planning is efficient and much more effective than waiting to see what the buyer says.

What to do about gate-keepers

Question: What is the best way to deal with gate-keepers?
Answer: Gate-keepers must be treated in an authoritative, business-like manner.

Gate-keepers should not be considered as obstacles to be overcome. They are employed by companies to direct callers to the right person or department. Usually, it is unlikely that the gate-keeper has any attitude at all towards new suppliers making a prospecting call. There is simply a job of work to be done. The name or buying function of the person to be contacted is given to the gate-keeper, who then either puts the caller through or lets the caller know when the buyer can be contacted:

'No. I am sorry. Mr Wright is the buyer for lubricants and he is abroad until the end of next week. His secretary is off sick. Please telephone her at the end of the week and if she is back at work she will help you.'

It serves no purpose to 'sell' to gate-keepers. The gate-keeper may have the time of day to chat, but this is unlikely to contribute to getting an appointment. Simple questions are all that are needed:

'I want to speak to the buyer of lubricants, please. By the way, what is the gentleman's name?'

The secretary hurdle

Question: What is the best way of getting past secretaries?
Answer: To get past a buyer's secretary, the caller should reflect authority and a manner of total confidence.

Whether calling in person or telephoning, there is no substitute for a confident manner and speaking voice. The caller's real feelings may be nervousness, shyness and apprehension but the person being spoken to must not detect this. He or she must believe that there is total confidence. On the telephone, the voice, the manner and what is said are the only signals. These signals must therefore convey a pleasant but positive manner.

It is not good policy to be impolite. It is important, however, to *tell* rather than to *ask*, wherever possible. The secretary cannot be ordered to do anything but she is told to ask for an appointment, rather than asked if she would be willing to try to obtain one. It is a question of authority. Those who do not have natural authority must acquire it. It takes practice, but authority can be learned:

'Hello. My name is Gorringe of Brent Glass Ltd. I want to show the buyer our new spring range. Please ask him for an appointment for this week. I am available on Tuesday or Thursday, whichever is convenient.'

'Hello. This is Brent Glass Ltd. My name is John Gorringe. I would like you to tell the buyer that our new spring range is ready. This week I am available on Tuesday or Thursday. Please ask him for an appointment on one of those days.'

Buyers have authority to buy. Secretaries do not. It is wrong to sell to secretaries although the temptation is often there. When the secretary asks the reason for wanting to see the buyer, the answer must always be given in general terms. Specific details of colours, sizes and prices are of value to the buyer but they should not be given to the secretary. As little as possible should be said to the secretary as the following reasons show:

1   If details of the caller's exciting offer are relayed by the secretary to the buyer, they may be presented out of context.
2   There is a danger of important aspects of the offer getting distorted.
3   The true benefits, set against the buyer's special needs, may be lost.

   Secretary   'What do you want to see Mr Wethered about? He is tied up at the moment.'
   Caller   'We have a range of American fittings that are new to this country.'

There is a deliberate silence after the short answer. Anything further leads to a discussion of the product and the objective of the call is to discuss the product with the buyer, Mr Wethered. If the secretary persists with her questions, the caller must be equally firm, but never rude or condescending.

> *Secretary* 'What do you want to see Mr Wethered about? He is tied up at the moment.'
> *Caller* 'We have a range of American fittings that are new to this country.'
> *Secretary* 'In what way are the fittings new?'
> *Caller* 'The new product items are very exciting and successful. What time will the buyer be free?'

The absent buyer

Question: What should be done when the buyer is out?
Answer: Find out exactly when the buyer is returning. Leave the name of the caller and state the time when a call back will be made.

If the buyer is out, the call must still be put to good use. It is counter-productive simply to ring off. Leads are precious, no matter how long the prospective customer list is at the particular time of the call. The time at which the buyer is going to be available is established by asking:

> *Telephonist* 'Hello. I am sorry to have kept you waiting. I am afraid that Mr Bentine is out.'
> *Caller* 'Oh, what a pity. Please tell me what time Mr Bentine is coming back.'
> *Telephonist* 'Mr Bentine should be in after four o'clock.'
> *Caller* 'Right, could you please tell Mr Bentine that Mr Brendon called and will be calling back at four-fifteen. Thank you. Goodbye.'

It is customary for people to call buyers. When presented with a message that someone has telephoned, the buyer considers whether the name is known. Is it someone recently met? Is it a person with whose company there is already a business relationship? It is a buyer's professional responsibility to know suppliers and personnel within his or her field.

When there is subsequent contact at 4.15 p.m. the buyer remembers the message that was left. It is easier for the caller too.

'Oh yes, Mr Brendon, I had a message that you would call back.'

That statement is much warmer and friendlier than:

'Mr Bentine speaking. What can I do for you?'

When the buyer is out there is another option, which is for the caller to leave his or her name and telephone number. If, acting on the message, the buyer does call back, the caller is in a very strong position. The situation is even better for the caller than being put straight through to a buyer in a conventional prospecting call. When a buyer calls back, he or she has had to make a specific effort to do so and the prospecting caller has the total attention of the buyer – for as long as it can be held.

When a name and telephone number are left by a caller, preparation must be made to receive incoming calls. Prospecting calls need to be made with a script and the total concentration of the caller and care must be taken to ensure that a buyer calling back does not catch the caller unawares.

Sometimes buyers do not call unknown callers back. If a message is left for an absent buyer, the initiative no longer belongs to the caller. If the buyer does not call back, an effort must be made to make contact a second time. When the caller actually speaks to the buyer he or she can make slight capital from referring to the first call and the message that was left. The buyer is in the wrong for not having paid the courtesy of calling back. However, professional buyers develop very 'thick skins' and it is unlikely that the advantage will be sustained for more than a moment.

The right form of greeting

Question: What is the best way of introducing oneself?
Answer: If the caller's company is very famous, state the company name first and then the caller's name. Otherwise simply give the caller's own name.

First impressions should be good impressions. An introduction must be precise and informative. There are two distinct introductory situations:

Situation 1   The caller is talking to a gate-keeper, a receptionist or a secretary.

It should not really matter if the caller is a lord or a dustman. Once the name has been obtained, it is going to be passed on to the buyer. If the name is announced clearly and authoritatively, it is 'ready' for passing on. The courtesy title of Mr or Mrs – or any other title – should be added. In a small way it depersonalizes the conversation and contributes to the authority of the caller.

If the caller's company is not well known and it is not of paramount importance that the company name is communicated immediately, it should not be given at the same time as the caller's own name. Two unknown names do not give an advantage over one unknown name.

Situation 2   The caller is talking to a buyer.

The caller gives his or her surname or first name and surname. Either is acceptable, so it is a matter of personal choice. If the company is famous – for example Shell, British Oxygen Company, Ford Motor Company – the caller may wish to give that instead to be sure of securing at least initial interest. Mr, Mrs or Miss is a courtesy title and the caller does not use it. Others will add a courtesy title when the caller's name is used. However, protocol relaxes when ladies are involved and if the caller feels more comfortable adding Mrs or Miss to her name, this is acceptable. The same situation arises with 'Dr'. The United Kingdom is currently more formal than some countries. In America and in Australia first name terms are adopted in business circles on first meeting, or in the first conversation. This does not happen in the United Kingdom to a very great extent.

Examples

'Mr Bartholomew? This is British Oxygen. I am calling because. . . .'
'Mr Bartholomew? British Oxygen Company. My name is Taylor. I am calling because . . . .'
'Mr Bartholomew? Good morning. My name is David Taylor of British Oxygen. I am calling because. . . .'

Useful opening gambits

Question: What is the best way to start the conversation with the buyer?

Answer: First, an introduction is made. A reason for calling, designed to arouse strong interest in the buyer, follows.

When telephoning for an appointment, two *Golden rules* apply. The first is *Golden rule* 1: always smile when speaking to the prospective customer. It is desirable that the caller is relaxed and comfortable. The second rule is *Golden rule* 5: always aim at achieving the objectives.

Padding out the call by way of social chat is counter-productive. While the caller has the buyer's attention he or she must take advantage of the opportunity. There are certain situations that are attractive to every buyer:

1 The buyer is the first in the market with a product.
2 The buyer's goods are the most competitive in price.
3 The buyer has exclusive distribution rights for certain products.
4 The buyer is able to offer prestigious products.
5 The buyer is able to offer products for which there is strong demand.

Any call leading to the satisfaction of one or more of these situations should find the buyer receptive to a request for an appointment.

Examples

Gambit 1   An innovative product.

'Mr Hoskins, my name is John Kemp of United Technol Limited. We have a range of models that are quite new to this country. The technology is different from anything used before. May I show them to you next week?'

Gambit 2   A competitively priced product.

'Mr Hoskins, my name is John Kemp of United Technol Limited. We have a range of models at prices that are the lowest in the market. May I show them to you next week?'

Gambit 3   Exclusive distribution rights.

'Mr Hoskins, we have divided the country into regions and we are now appointing exclusive distributors for our range. May I show you our products next week?'

Gambit 4   The 'halo' effect of a prestigious product.

'Mr Hoskins, my name is John Kemp of United Technol Limited. We are currently doing business with Ferranti and Racal. May I show you our range of models next week, for you to assess whether they would be of interest?'

Gambit 5   A product that is much in demand.

'Mr Hoskins, my name is John Kemp of United Technol Limited. We have a range of models that have been extremely successful in the north and west of England. I will be in London next Tuesday and am staying until Thursday. May I call on you during that period?'

A point arises from gambit 5 that is worth noting. When a company's location is distant from the buyer's own office, there is, occasionally, a reluctance to invite a representative of the company to make a special long journey. Demonstration appointments carry no obligations but, nonetheless, slight moral pressures are created. To avoid this, buyers are less likely to make casual appointments with unknown companies some distance away. When a caller telephones a buyer who is a long way away, care should be taken not to suggest that a special journey is being made.

Dealing with refusal

Question: What should be done when the buyer says 'No' to an appointment?'

Answer: Identify the reason for the refusal. Pave the way for a future appointment.

When a buyer says 'No' to a request for an appointment there are a numbei of reasons why he or she may do so:

Reasons for saying 'No'

Budget exhausted   The monies allocated for the season, or month or whatever time unit is adopted by the company, are spent. Many buyers have an ad hoc account to take advantage of special situations. If a buyer's budget has genuinely been used up, the benefits promised by the caller have to be very special to persuade the buyer to dip into reserve funds.

> *Buyer*   'No, I am sorry Mr Cross. Your merchandise sounds attractive but I have spent my budget for this season. Contact me in the autumn.'
>
> *Caller*   'I see, Mrs White. I am sorry to hear that we are too late. I have not told you yet that we are mounting a co-ordinated press and television advertising campaign to launch our products. If you were a stockist, it might be possible to include your company name in the press advertisements. Our promotions last year were extremely successful. May I show you the range next week?'

No time   At certain times of the year buyers are particularly busy people. When the buyer's programme is full the possibility of changing a 'No' to a 'Yes' is remote.

It is important, however, that the buyer has some reminder of the caller's interest. A short letter is suitable and, where literature is available, it should be sent.

Mrs Joan White
Fashion Accessories Buyer
Harrods Ltd
London SW1

Dear Mrs White

re: CICOGNA Italian Silk Headsquares

We spoke today on the telephone and I invited you to see the beautiful range of CICOGNA squares, at our showroom or in your department. Sadly, you told me that your diary is full for the next three weeks.

The CICOGNA squares have had considerable success in comparable departmental stores in many European capitals.

I will telephone you again at the beginning of next month to see if there is a convenient time for us to meet.

Yours sincerely

Satisfied with existing suppliers This problem is a difficult one. When a buyer has success with a supplier's merchandise, loyalties develop. The buyer works closely with the supplier in getting the merchandise 'right' and, when emergencies arise, the relationship makes sure that solutions are found.

A caller trying to open an account with a buyer who is well serviced by all suppliers has an uphill task. Emphasis must be placed on extra benefits. These benefits are likely to be:

High profitability
Free advertising publicity
Total or partial contribution towards special promotion activities
Merchandise on a sale or return basis

Straightforward blandishment of ordinary product benefits is unlikely to be successful in generating an appointment.

Change of buying personnel A new buyer is usually very cautious when taking over a buying function. A minimum commitment with the existing 'bread and butter' suppliers is placed while the buyer absorbs the trends and idiosyncrasies of customer purchases. An account controlled by a new buyer is an ideal one to open. The new buyer's broom is busy sweeping out any faults that have been inherited. At the same time the buyer is anxious to consolidate relationships with suppliers whose merchandise is successful and to introduce fresh merchandise that will sell well. If the caller can get in with his or her new goods, there are exciting possibilities for future business. All stops must therefore be pulled out to get the initial order.

> *Buyer* 'No, I am sorry Mr Cross, I have just taken over the buying for this department. I am not ready to see any new suppliers. Contact me again next season.'
> *Caller* 'Oh, Mrs Brown, I understand the problem if you have just taken over the department. I am sure that you need to see all the existing suppliers first. There is one point. We are carrying a special range of silk squares, designed for us by Gucci by a special arrangement. We have the publicity pulls from the fashion magazines in France, Germany and Italy.

There has been enormous success in Europe. Should you not see the range now, so that when you are ready to buy you will know whether it is right for your department? I could call and see you tomorrow?'

Paving the way by letter

Question: Should one always write to the buyer before tele-phoning?

Answer: No. A letter is often helpful in giving confidence to the caller but it is not effective in terms of cost or time for the caller to write before every call.

Telephoning an unknown buyer for an appointment is difficult for many people. There is a nasty feeling in the pit of the stomach as the telephone is picked up. The problem is not restricted to in-experienced people. Some of the most successful sales people in the field balk at cold canvass by telephone – until they have been taught the techniques.

In a face-to-face situation there are many signals going back-wards and forwards between the two parties. Some signals are verbal but many are not. On the telephone there are no non-verbal signals. The caller is therefore performing in a restricted environ-ment and this explains the apprehension that goes hand in hand with telephone prospecting. The caller has a subconscious fear of being inadequate because the familiar non-verbal signals that stimulate the caller's efficient reactions are not there. The caller is uncertain what the response to his or her words are.

Writing a letter first provides the caller with a path through that area of uncertainty. The caller has lost his or her anonymity.

'Mr Winfield, my name is Robert Thomas of Associated Conduits Ltd. I wrote to you last week. Did you receive our letter?'

Mr Robert Thomas has an identity previously announced in his letter. His initial verbal contact with Mr Winfield is in respect of a matter in which he knows the major facts – the letter which was sent. Whether or not the letter arrived is not threatening to Mr Thomas. It is a fact that will be disclosed by Mr Winfield.

The hurdle to be overcome by callers lies in the opening meeting of voices at the beginning of the call. This is where the letter written in advance is so helpful.

The resources needed to write letters are considerable. They are:

A secretary to type the letters
Headed paper, carbon paper and copy paper
A typewriter
Envelopes and postage
Rental of secretary's office space
Contingent cost of other letters not typed
Time involved

Paving the way with a letter before each call is attractive but the caller must decide whether the letter is warranted in the light of all the costs and in the light of the time needed for the letters to be produced. With limited exceptions the letter is of real value only until the caller becomes proficient in using the telephone effectively. The exceptions are associated with certain prestigious and long established companies where callers must comply with tradition and make written application before any sales meetings will be contemplated.

Summary

Questions	Answers
1 When trying to make an appointment who does one ask to speak to?	One asks to speak to the buyer by name or by buying function.
2 When put through to the buyer, what is said to confirm that it is the buyer speaking?	A direct question of confirmation is asked, so that the prospecting call may proceed.
3 What questions find out if the buyer is interested?	There are five questions that the caller uses, each of which is designed to elicit a specific reply. The appropriate questions to use are planned in advance.
4 What is the best way to deal with gate-keepers?	Gate-keepers must be treated in an authoritative, business-like manner.
5 What is the best way of getting past secretaries?	To get past a buyer's secretary, the caller should reflect authority and a manner of total confidence.
6 What should be done when the buyer is out?	Find out exactly when the buyer is returning. Leave the name of the caller and state the time when a call back will be made.
7 What is the best way of introducing oneself?	If the caller's company is very famous, state the company name first and then the caller's name. Otherwise simply give the caller's own name.
8 What is the best way to start the conversation with the buyer?	First, an introduction is made. A reason for calling, designed to arouse strong interest in the buyer, follows.
9 What should be done when the buyer says 'No' to an appointment?	Identify the reason for the refusal. Pave the way for a future appointment.
10 Should one always write to the buyer before telephoning?	No. Letters are not effective in terms of cost or time (See page 59.)

Chapter 3

How to match benefits to needs

Before reading this chapter, answer the questions first. Testing your knowledge identifies any areas that may need particular attention. The answers are summarized at the end of the chapter.

Questions

1 How are customer needs identified?
2 Is there more than one kind of benefit message?
3 Is there a technique for passing benefit messages?
4 Is there a method of finding out how near one is to a sale?
5 What is to be done if the benefit messages do not produce a sale?

Answers

Chapter 3 How to match benefits to needs

Knowing what the customer wants – Different kinds of benefit messages – Saying it right – How to know when one is winning – Meeting brick walls – Summary

Knowing what the customer wants

Question: How are customer needs identified?
Answer: Needs are identified by listening and by questioning. In a one-to-one meeting observation plays a part too.

Operating rule 2 for telephone prospecting explains the customer need. Together with wants, needs are the motivating forces that lead a customer to make a buying decision. A need is something that a customer must have for his or her everyday activities to continue. A want is what a customer would like to have. Selling against wants is an uphill task. A sale depends on matching benefits to needs which is why customer needs are so important.

In a telephone conversation the customer may announce a need requirement immediately:

Customer 'Hello, is that the Parkinson Valet service?'
Receptionist 'Yes.'
Customer 'I need invisible mending. I have just torn my new evening dress. Do you do invisible mending?'

Or, when the caller telephones a prospective customer, explaining his or her own expertise in the process of introduction, the customer may be motivated to declare a pressing need. Listening carefully is productive in less straightforward situations. The caller must be ready to probe with questions any avenue of possible need introduced by the customer:

Caller 'Am I speaking to the managing director?'

Customer 'Yes. Mr Crossland here.'

Caller 'Mr Crossland, my name is Ben Torky. I have just joined North Street Motors. I am telephoning to introduce myself. We are only two blocks away but there does not appear to be any record in our company of contact with you. May I ask what car you are driving?'

Customer 'Mr Torky, I am not receptive to any discussion on motor cars at the present time. On the way to my office I have just dented the front of my new Jaguar.'

Caller 'Mr Crossland, I am sorry. Look, we are not in the car hire business but we do maintain a small fleet of cars for our service customers. As we are so near, would it be of help to you, now, if we made a hire car available?'

Sometimes prospective customers are cagey about their needs. They answer curtly and reluctantly and discourage conversation. Immediate neutral open questions are required to extract information on areas of need.

Different kinds of benefit message

Question: Is there more than one kind of benefit message?

Answer: Yes. There are two major kinds of benefit message. One is a product knowledge statement. The other is a selling benefit message.

A benefit message is a statement, so called because it describes advantages and benefits – real or potential.

'Product knowledge' benefit statements

Such statements are used in the early part of a prospecting call or sales presentation when the scene is being set. For example: 'The car reaches sixty miles per hour from a standing start in ten seconds.' The acceleration of many cars is not as fast so this is a positive fact differentiating the particular car in one aspect from other cars. The statement is a benefit statement when it is addressed to someone concerned with the comparative qualities of different makes of cars. When the statement is made to someone who has no interest in cars, the statement carries no benefit. The words and meaning are understood but that is all. There is no benefit.

To give another example: 'The publication has a certified circulation of two million readers.' To a potential advertiser, the words carry meaning and something more. If the potential advertiser were to advertise, a certain attractive level of response could be expected.

In the early part of a telephone conversation the caller gives a lot of information:

Who it is that is calling.
The nature of the product or service being offered.
What is wanted by the caller.

Not all of the information can be classified as forming benefit messages and it is unlikely that any of the benefit messages in the opening stages will directly result in a sale. The product knowledge benefit statements are factual and describe product qualities and functions. Other examples are:

'This lever opens the window.'
'The covers are made in nylon to give harder wearing.'
'The ventilation system is operated by simple manual control.'

'Selling' benefit messages

It is the selling benefit messages that get results. The statements satisfy the major needs of the buyer. The selling benefit messages provided are factual, or true, as with product knowledge statements, but they also have a 'plus'. They emphasize and magnify the advantages over other products and services. Selling benefit messages, which are used to close sales, refer to the *function* of the product or service and not merely the component parts.

Ernest Dichter, who is an authority on motivational research, writes of shoe manufacturers selling 'beautiful feet' not shoes, and he describes the cosmetics manufacturers as selling 'hope' not lipstick.

There are many more examples. The customer buying a new car does not buy a prefabricated assemblage of component parts of high quality, fitted with an internal combustion engine. He or she buys reliability, status, dependability, comfort or economy.

'In addition to the magnificent display case we guarantee that our cooking knives retain their razor sharpness for three years. Who else can make that claim, Mr Johnson? Will you take a sample order of twenty-five sets?'

Saying it right

Question: Is there a technique for passing benefit messages?
Answer: Yes. Product knowledge benefit statements are given explicitly, and usually a number of product knowledge statements are given together. For the selling benefit messages there are five separate stages.

In the telephone call or the face-to-face presentation there are five steps to giving a selling benefit statement. In most cases the benefit message is an answer to a prospective customer's question or statement. The early part of the conversation has described the caller's product or service factually. The customer's needs have been qualified and the customer has started the decision-making process and is gathering specific information.

Five steps to passing a selling benefit message

1 Pause, or repeat the question or statement. This gives a moment to think.
2 Give the benefit statement describing the product or service *function*.
3 Provide reasons why the benefits are true.
4 Summarize what has been said.
5 Obtain the commitment of the customer to accepting the validity and relevance of the benefit statement.

Example

A motor car dealership is prospecting for business for a new turbo model. In the course of the telephone conversation the question is asked: '. . . and what is the acceleration?'

> 'The acceleration? The turbo reaches one hundred miles per hour from a standing start in ten seconds. Not only do you get a wonderful sensation of speed, but you are taken out of any awkward situation very quickly indeed.
>
> 'Turbo-charging gives an added dimension of power. On the grounds of safety and performance the turbo is a most attractive car. Do you not agree that safety and performance are two of the really important requirements of a car these days?'

The pattern is not rigid. The benefit statement does not always have to be formulated in exactly the given sequence of stages to be effective. What is important is that the benefit *functions* are perceived and understood by the prospective customer. It is not sufficient that the customer merely hears them.

How to know when one is winning

Question: Is there a method of finding out how near one is to a sale?

Answer: Trial close questions show whether or not one is on the right lines.

In the face-to-face situation there are many non-verbal signals given – a smile – a nod – the head bent towards the speaker – the prospective customer moves nearer. These signals are valuable feedback. They indicate that there is interest and that benefits are matching needs. Other signals indicate alarm, or lack of interest – fidgeting – coughing – the pupils of the eye open wide – the prospective customer moves back or away – the head shakes.

On the telephone none of this is seen. There are only voice inflections, changes in tempo and changes in manner. A yardstick is therefore needed to measure progress.

Questioning techniques are used. A trial close is made. The neutral closed question, which is of minimal value in the qualification process, helps enormously here. It summarizes the position. A 'Yes' or 'No' answer from the prospective customer clearly shows whether there is progress:

'Am I right?'
'Do you like it?'
'Is it the right colour?'
'Will it be suitable?'
'Will it fit?'
'Is it fast enough?'

If the answer is 'No' the benefit messages are not matching the real needs which probably means that the needs are not yet qualified correctly. The neutral leading question should therefore follow:

Caller   'Is it the right colour?'
Customer   'No.'
Caller   'What would the right colour be?'

Or, alternatively:

Caller   'Is it fast enough for you?'
Customer   'No.'
Caller   'What is the speed level you need?'

Meeting brick walls

Question: What is to be done if the benefit messages do not produce a sale?
Answer: Go back to square one. Identify the needs that the customer has. They are not necessarily the needs that he or she is presumed to have because of similar circumstances in the past.

When a person sells a product or service every day patterns of buying behaviour emerge. The major portion of the sales satisfy a few dominant needs and it is easy to think that if eight out of every hundred customers buy because of the same need, the next person will also buy for the same reason. However, the minority must not be forgotten. When trial closes fail it is necessary to rethink. A useful technique is to throw the problem back on the customer:

'Mrs Hislop, from what you are saying, the shower unit does not appear to be entirely right for you. The majority of our customers have said that what appealed to them about the particular model I demonstrated to you yesterday was its performance and economy. If you were to install that model what would be the reasons that made you realize it was right for you?'

Summary

Questions	Answers
1 How are customer needs identified?	Needs are identified by listening and by questioning. In a one-to-one meeting observation plays a part too.
2 Is there more than one kind of benefit message?	Yes. There are two major kinds of benefit message. One is a product knowledge statement. The other is a selling benefit message.
3 Is there a technique for passing benefit messages?	Yes. Product knowledge benefit statements are given explicitly, and usually a number of product knowledge statements are given together. For the selling benefit message there are five separate stages.
4 Is there a method of finding out how near one is to a sale?	Trial close questions show whether or not one is on the right lines.
5 What is to be done if the benefit messages do not produce a sale?	Go back to square one. Identify the needs that the customer has. They are not necessarily the needs that he or she is presumed to have because of similar circumstances in the past.

Chapter 4

How to overcome objections and win

Answer the following questions before reading this chapter. Check how many answers were correct from the checklist at the end of the chapter after reading the text. If any answers were wrong, have they been the cause of lost sales in the past?

Questions

1 Why do customers object?
2 What kinds of objection do customers raise?
3 What is the best method of preparing to meet objections?
4 What is the technique to be used in overcoming objections?
5 Why do customers argue?
6 What is the way to prevent arguments developing?
7 How do I stop getting angry at incompetence on the telephone?

Answers

Chapter 4 How to overcome objections and win

Reasons for objecting – Different ways of saying 'No' – Getting ready to win – Overcoming objections – The other side's point of view – Avoiding arguments – It's not my fault – Summary

Reasons for objecting

Question: Why do customers object?
Answer: There are three reasons why customers object:
1   The customer is not able to make a buying decision.
2   The customer has not been persuaded to buy.
3   The customer believes that there is a reason for the proposition to be invalid.

Countering a prospective customer's objections does not always lead to a sale, however great the expertise and skill used, because the objections may not be the real ones. A customer does not always like to admit that he or she is not in a position to buy. The customer says, instead:

'It's the wrong colour.'
'The shape is not right.'
'It's too expensive.'
'It seems to be too old fashioned.'

A convincing argument that the colour, shape, price or year of production are acceptable still does not get an order, if the customer does not have the authority to sign a buying order, or if there is insufficient money available.

If the customer has simply not been persuaded to buy, he or she will say something to reduce the pressure being put on them by the caller:

72

'It's the wrong colour.'
'The shape is not right.'

This is a red herring – the customer just wants to get away.

There are occasions when the customer is quite certain that what he or she is told is incorrect. The customer objects believing that he or she has right on their side. In the majority of cases this may be so but sometimes the facts are not as they seem.

Example

On two occasions in the last three months Tom Jefferies, the sales manager, has had cause to be in the 'Goods Inwards' section of the warehouse. Usually, there is no reason for him to be there. On each occasion a delivery from the same supplier was being unpacked and on both occasions Tom Jefferies heard the store-keeper complaining loudly that the delivery was incomplete and the packing list wrong. Tom Jefferies therefore believes that every delivery from that particular supplier is faulty. He does not happen to know of the forty-one other deliveries that were exactly right.

Different ways of saying 'No'

Question: What kinds of objection do customers raise?
Answer: Customer objections mainly fall within well defined parameters such as cost, delivery, quality, etc.

A commercial sale is a link in a chain of contributory activities:

Pricing
Product characteristics – quality, shape, size, weight, colour, density, viscosity, etc.
Promotional activities – packaging, advertising, point of sale material, PR
Delivery times
Distribution channels
Production capacity
Personal selling
Personnel
Service capability – pre-sale and post-sale

Training
Customer interest
Customer stock levels
Customer resources -- time, money, storage, personnel
Customer loyalty
Technical resources

The list is not exhaustive but it is useful as a framework from which to classify the types of customer objections, for example:

Pricing objection:	'It is too expensive.'
Training objection:	'It is too difficult for the oper-atives to use correctly.'
Customer loyalty objection:	'I have always found Whacko satisfactory.'

When the nature of a customer objection is correctly identified, the problem of dealing with that objection is simplified.

Getting ready to win

Question: What is the best method of preparing to meet objections?

Answer: Before commencing the first sales call, thorough preparation must be made of appropriate answers to all the likely objections to be met. Waiting to deal with any objections as they arise puts the caller at a disadvantage.

A few fortunate people think very quickly on their feet. The majority arrive at a marvellous answer on the way home, when it is too late. Thorough preparation may seem tedious but it is well worthwhile. Before making the call prepare a grid on a large sheet of paper and enter three column headings as shown in Figure 7. The column headings are:

Objection type

In the left-hand column list all of the objection types likely to be met for the particular product or service concerned. Not all of the items listed above necessarily apply but others, not given, may be relevant.

Objection type	Likely objections	Responses
Pricing	It is too expensive ? What is its value ? We don't have that much money. Would we get the money back when the house is sold ? Is there a cheaper type of construction ?	What is being compared ? On a square metre basis a loft conversion is substantially cheaper than a ground floor extension. How is the convenience of an extra bedroom, or a playroom for the children evaluated ? When the house is up for sale an extra room makes it much more desirable and easy to sell. etc.

Figure 7   *Format for preparing to meet any objections that arise*

Likely objections

In the second column enter every possible objection falling within the objection type.

Response

In the third column enter every type of response to the objections.

Preparing all the possible responses is slow and tedious but it is an activity designed to help the caller with his or her sales call. It must be stressed that knowing a correct response to an objection is not the same as countering that objection. Customers must be treated diplomatically. The first step is to establish all the possible responses to an objection. How to deal with those responses is set out in Chapter 5.

Summit Loft Conversions Ltd is a building company specializing in converting the loft space of private dwellings into habitable accommodation. Apart from recommendations by clients, business is obtained from advertisements placed in the national and local press. Additionally, blanket canvassing campaigns are carried out with drop-cards pushed through letter boxes.

Using the grid shown in Figure 7 preparation is made to counter the objections likely to be met when prospective customers make contact. Each objection type is considered in turn:

Pricing objection

Likely objections

1   It is too expensive?
2   What is its value?
3   We don't have that much money.
4   Would we get the money back when the house is sold?
5   Is there a cheaper type of construction?

Responses

1   What is being compared? On a square metre basis a loft conversion is substantially cheaper than a ground floor extension.
2   How is the convenience of an extra bedroom or a playroom for the children evaluated? When the house is up for sale an extra room makes it much more desirable and easy to sell.
3   There are HP facilities – so the payments may be spread over five years.
4   Divide the number of living-rooms in this property, not counting the kitchen and bathroom, into the present market value to give a value for each living-room. That value is much more than the proposed cost of the conversion.
5   It is possible to skimp a little with some materials – soft wood window sills – dispensing with ceiling cornices – lowest quality door furniture. However, there are statutory requirements by the local authorities in terms of construction and insulation.

Product characteristic objection

Likely objections

1   The roof will be too low.
2   A sloping roof is not suitable.

76

3   The water tank and expansion tank are in the way.
4   The roof space is used for storage.
5   There is no room for a staircase.
6   The gurgling of the water tank will make sleep impossible.
7   You will not get your materials up because our staircase is too narrow.
8   There is a wasp's nest there.

Responses

1   There is a statutory requirement for an internal ceiling height of 2 metres. Allowing for flooring joists, ceiling joists, boarding and insulation, there only needs to be a distance of about 2.3 metres from existing joists to the highest internal point.
2   The sloping roof is cut away and a mansard roof or dormer windows are built in.
3   The water tanks and pipes are resited by our plumbers.
4   Not all of the roof space is used. An access door or doors can be built into the walls. Floorboards will be laid in the unused parts of the loft space to help storage.
5   The staircase is built up over the existing staircase through the landing ceiling. None of the bedrooms are disturbed.
6   The walls of the loft room are well insulated. If required, there can be extra insulation.
7   The materials are hoisted up the outside of the house. Materials are taken in through the hole in the roof that we cut for the windows.
8   For us, removing a wasp's nest is a simple task and any holes found in the eaves or roof are automatically mended.

Promotional activities objection

Not relevant.

Delivery time objection

Likely objections

1 We need the room by Easter time when a relative is coming to stay from Australia.
2 I cannot stay away from work for so long, to look after the builders.
3 Crisscross Loft Conversions have quoted a start in ten days' time.
4 What guarantee is there that you will finish in that time?
5 What happens if the material suppliers keep you waiting?

Responses

1 If it is particularly urgent we will ask another client if they will exchange starting dates with you.
2 It is not necessary for anyone to be in the house. The men are trustworthy and have been with our company for a long time. We can get in and out through the roof.
3 We have built one hundred and three conversions in this neighbourhood alone. We believe that Crisscross Loft Conversions are short of work.
4 Our reputation is at stake. We rely on satisfying you with our work for recommendation to other clients.
5 There is always a buffer stock of timbers in our yard. Once a contract is closed with a client the materials are ordered immediately.

Distribution channels objection

Not relevant.

Production capacity objection

Likely objections

1   Terrible stories of jobs dragging on and on.
2   What guarantee is there that the roof will not fall in?
3   If it rains whilst the roof is open the house will get soaked.
4   The new room will be higher than the central heating system, so it will be freezing in the winter time.
5   It is only possible to work in the summer time, otherwise the house would become too cold.

Responses

1   The carpenters and the plumbers are the company's own staff, so there is full control. The men will not move onto another job until they have finished their work.
2   The staff are competent workmen. No supporting timbers are ever cut unless adequate reinforcement has been installed.
3   There are tarpaulins to cover every opening. One option is to build, at extra cost, a permanent umbrella of corrugated sheeting supported by scaffolding and enclosed by tarpaulin.
4   If there is sufficient height to accommodate the expansion tank above the ceiling of the loft room, the central heating system can be extended. Otherwise electrically powered heating is possible.
5   The holes cut in the roof are not left open for long periods. If the weather is very cold, the openings will be covered up all the time except when materials are going in and out.

Personal selling objection

Not relevant.

Personnel objection

Likely objections

Personnel incompetent or insensitive to other people's property – might steal.

Response

Personnel are directly employed and known for some time. They are known to be trustworthy.

Service capability objection

Likely objection

What guarantees are offered against defective workmanship?

Response

The conversions are guaranteed by the company for a period of five years.

Training objection

Not applicable.

Customer interest objection

Likely objections

1 I will think about it.
2 We would prefer to move to somewhere larger.
3 We would rather have the extension on the ground floor.
4 Spending that much will take the value of this house above the market level.

Responses

1   What is it that you will think about? Materials are going up in price next month. Enlarging the home is much less expensive than moving. Children are settled.
2   Carefully examine the cost of moving house – financial and emotional.
3   The converted loft is cheaper and less noisy.
4   The extra room gives the house a unique selling point when it is time to move. In the meantime, how does one cost the advantage of additional living space and comfort?

Customer stock levels objection

Not relevant.

Customer resources objection

Likely objections

Cannot afford it and many other objections similar to those in the *Pricing* objection.

Responses

Same as responses to *Pricing* objections.

Customer loyalty objection

Likely objection

Crisscross Loft Conversions converted the loft in our last home.

Response

How long is it since the work was done? We have become very strong in the last twelve years. We have built over two thousand conversions in this borough alone. Would you like to inspect our work?

Technical objection

Likely objection

Quality and reliability of workmanship.

Response

Our work has to be approved by the local authority Building Inspector during building and on completion.

Overcoming objections

Question: What is the technique to be used in overcoming objections?
Answer: There are three simple steps:
    1 Repeat prospective customer's objections.
    2 Eliminate all other objections.
    3 Neutralize the objection.

Customer objections are hurdles to be overcome. Objections are met in all types of telephone calls. Wherever possible, the objection that is met should be turned to the caller's advantage. It is important, however, that the objection is identified as being the correct one. Otherwise the caller meets further resistance,

Simple steps to overcoming objections

Step 1   Repeat the objection

There is double value here. Firstly, there is time to think. Secondly, the customer hears the objection raised, isolated from the context of his or her own attitudes and words.

Step 2   Eliminate all other objections

A point-blank question is effective: 'Is this your only objection?'. Alternatively, without being so direct:

'I am not sure that I fully understand what you are saying. Would you explain more fully?'

Step 3   Neutralize the objection

There are a number of ways of doing this;
(a)   *Throwback method*   The actual objection is used as a selling point. A different perspective is given to the customer by changing the frame of reference:

Customer   'I am not sure that I like the hatchback model.'
Dealer   'National figures show that the hatchback is the fastest selling of all cars this year.'

Not only is the objection countered, but the prospective customer is made to feel secure.
(b)   *Comparison with competitive products*   The benefits are compared with those of the competition. The examples chosen show the competition at a real disadvantage:

Customer   'The cost of a display advertisement in this wall planner guide seems very expensive.'
Producer   'Ten thousand guides are distributed for us through a Dun and Bradstreet mailing list. Do you know of any other producer offering this certified distribution? Considering the distribution the advertisement costs are very cheap. Will you participate?'

(c)   *'Yes, but . . .'*   Before demonstrating that the client is wrong the situation is defused by initial agreement:

Customer   'I have heard that at high speed the system becomes unstable.'

Manufacturer 'Yes, I can understand your caution. But we have tested the product to destruction. We will guarantee that there is no design fault.'

(d) *The lock close* The commitment of the prospective customer to buy is obtained, on condition that the objection is shown to be unfounded:

Customer 'The colour of the kettle seems wrong. I prefer it in red.'

Supplier 'I am sure that I can supply you with a red kettle. If I can, will you buy it?'

Customer 'I don't really like dralon. I prefer leather upholstery.'

Upholsterer 'If I am able to supply that armchair upholstered in leather, will you buy it?'

The lock close is extremely effective. When all of the objections have been identified and eliminated bar one, the removal of the final objection leaves the customer with nowhere to go. When the lock close does not work, it usually means that other objections exist which have not been disclosed.

Example

Manufacturer 'Hello, madam. I am calling about the orthopaedic bed you inspected yesterday in the showroom. What did you think of it?'

Customer 'Oh yes. I had to leave before I had a chance to talk to you again. The bed – I found it too hard.'

Manufacturer 'You found it too hard?''

Customer 'Yes. I did not expect a soft mattress, but it seemed very hard indeed. Too hard.

Manufacturer 'I am not sure that I understand. There has to be support for the back condition that you said you had?'

Customer 'Yes. But I am concerned that if the bed is too hard it will do as much damage as if it were too soft.'

Manufacturer 'Oh, that is certainly an important question. Is that your only concern about the bed?'

Customer 'Yes.'

Manufacturer 'Well, all of our beds are manufactured to the medical specification prepared by our consultant orthopaedic surgeon. If I guarantee that your custom-built bed is manufactured to the degree of hardness specifically corresponding to your medical condition, will you buy it?'

The other side's point of view

Question: Why do customers argue?
Answer: Customers do not like to be contradicted, especially by strangers.

Telephoning a prospective customer invariably interrupts an activity. As the caller speaks, he or she is establishing credibility and neutralizing the interruption. This is in addition to all the other activities of qualifying the prospective customer, making offers and guiding the conversation towards a sale. There is no background relationship of friendship to allow for a difference of opinion and if the caller persists in maintaining his or her stance, an argument results. The caller then has a problem because the premise on which the route to a sale is founded is one with which the caller disagrees.

Avoiding arguments

Question: What is the way to prevent arguments developing?
Answer: The caller must make a conscious effort to avoid an actual dispute. Every disagreement must be resolved in an indirect manner.

To telephone effectively, the caller must make a controlled effort to be tolerant. Arguments must be avoided at all costs. Whether an argument is won or lost, once it starts, the focus of the conversation moves. An emotional climate is set up which distorts the prospective customer's attitudes that lead to the buying decision. An argument introduces psychological barriers and invariably they stand in the way of objectives being reached.

The 'Yes, but . . .' method

A customer is never contradicted. If a customer says something on the telephone that is known to be untrue, the 'Yes, but . . .' method is adopted. First of all, the caller agrees with the statement. Contradiction generates a defensive position in the customer. Counter-arguments can then be made in a constructive way:

Customer 'We have decided not to buy that machine because spare parts will be unobtainable. The government has stopped all imports.'

Merchant 'Oh, yes. I see. But are you sure that your information is correct? May I ask where you obtained the information that all imports are being stopped?'

The caller knows that the Government has imposed a ban on certain categories of imports. The caller is quite sure on this point because it is necessary business procedure to know all regulations that affect the trading position. What the customer has said is nonsense but if the customer is told that the statement made is nonsense, he or she is going to be offended.

It's not my fault

Question: How do I stop getting angry at incompetence on the telephone?

Answer: Play the Squares Game to develop a better tolerance.

For the person who does a lot of telephoning and telephone selling there are many occasions when it is difficult not to get angry. It may be the telephonist at fault, or there may be other problems, for example:

The caller clearly states the name of the person wanted but the call is put through to someone else.

The caller is connected in the midst of describing his or her requirements.

The caller is cut off.

The number is interminably engaged.

The caller is left waiting and waiting.

The operator does not answer.

It is quite normal for a caller to want to throw the telephone at the operator but this must not happen! When things go wrong or the person at the other end of the telephone appears rather dense, the caller is in a frame of mind most conducive to argument.

The Squares Game

One way of maintaining sanity is to play the Squares Game. A separate page of a notebook for each day is all that is needed. Each time there has to be a real effort not to demolish the person at the other end of the telephone a small square is drawn. At the end of the day the squares are counted.

The daily total can be made competitive. Either the caller competes with himself or herself, or with colleagues who are also telephoning. The person with the lowest number of squares at the end of the day wins the kitty. This simple therapy really works. In psychological terms it is an effective catharsis. When telephone prospecting calls are made regularly it is found that the daily tally of squares gets smaller. With practice, the caller become more adept and, quite simply, as the telephone skills become more effective, the caller becomes more tolerant.

Summary

Questions	Answers
1 Why do customers object?	There are three reasons why customers object: 1 The customer is not able to make a buying decision. 2 The customer has not been persuaded to buy. 3 The customer believes that there is a reason for the proposition to be invalid.
2 What kinds of objection do customer raise?	Customer objections mainly fall within well defined parameters such as cost, delivery, quality, etc.
3 What is the best method of preparing to meet objections?	Before commencing the first sales call, thorough preparation must be made of appropriate answers to all the likely objections to be met. Waiting to deal with any objections as they arise puts the caller at a disadvantage.
4 What is the technique to be used in overcoming objections?	There are three simple steps: 1 Repeat prospective customer's objections. 2 Eliminate all other objections. 3 Neutralize the objection.
5 Why do customers argue?	Customers do not like to be contradicted, expecially by strangers.
6 What is the way to prevent arguments developing?	The caller must make a conscious effort to avoid an actual dispute. Every disagreement must be resolved in an indirect manner.
7 How do I stop getting angry at incompetence on the telephone?	Play the Squares Game to develop a better tolerance.

How to communicate on the phone

Answer the questions below before reading this chapter. The answers are collected together in summary at the end of the chapter.

Questions   **Answers**

1   What is meant by communi-
    cation?
2   When do customers mean
    what they say?
3   How are listening skills
    developed?
4   What are the best ways of
    answering customers' ques-
    tions?
5   What answers does the cus-
    tomer expect to hear?
6   What is the best time of day
    to make a call?
7   How long should the tele-
    phone call be?
8   How can telephone per-
    formance be improved?
9   How can the communication
    process be improved?

Chapter 5 How to communicate on the phone

Communicating – The customer story – Was something said? – Answering questions – The other point of view – Getting the timing right – When to stop talking – How to get better – Getting communication right – Summary

Communicating

Question: What is meant by communication?

Answer: In simple terms communication is the process of passing and receiving messages.

Communication is a process of passing messages. Message signals go from sender to receiver. At the same time, feedback or entirely different messages may be sent from the receiver to the sender. Third parties sometimes intrude and sometimes noise or external forces distort messages. Messages are not only words. Many signals are given before even the first words are uttered. The signals may take the form of a nervous cough, a gesture, a smile or fidgeting. For true communication all the available signals must be recognized.

Example The employment interview.
An applicant goes into the office of a prospective employer to be interviewed. Normally, in that situation the interviewer arranges for a chair for the applicant to sit on. The chair is placed in a position that is convenient for the interviewer and the interviewee. There is no value in the chair being a long way from the interviewer's desk because the applicant might not hear properly or it may be difficult for documents to be read. Similarly, if the chair is too close to the desk both parties feel crowded.

There are two options open to the interviewee:

1   The applicant is shown into the interviewer's office. When invited, he or she sits carefully and precisely on the chair. The applicant waits for the interview to begin.

This is reasonable behaviour and it is quite acceptable. It does not show the applicant to be weak and subservient. If anything, it suggests that the applicant is courteous and respectful.

2   The interviewee enters the room. When invited to sit down, he or she picks up the chair and moves it slightly into a new position, a few centimetres away. The applicant then sits comfortably and waits.

Up to that point, there is very little change in the physical situation. With this applicant, however, very much has been said without a word being uttered. By his or her action the applicant has given a body signal message that is very clear. The message is: 'Thank you for the interview situation. I welcome this meeting between us. I am going to listen to see if there can be a useful outcome. I have arranged myself comfortably. You may now go ahead.'

Communication messages do not have to be long and complicated. A sigh or an excited squeak tell as much as a long, prepared speech.

There is another example of non-verbal communication. It is demonstrated by an experiment carried out by the psychology department of an American university. The experimenters left coins in the slot of a cigarette vending machine sited on a busy shopping thoroughfare. Whenever a purchaser came to buy cigarettes it was not necessary to insert money because the correct coinage was already in the slot. When the purchase had been completed, the experimenter would go up as the buyer was leaving. The experimenter explained that he had used the machine just before. He had put his money in and then remembered that, from yesterday, he had stopped smoking. He had walked away angrily and had forgotten to take his money. He now remembered it and had returned to collect it.

The experiment was divided into two situations:

1   The experimenter courteously asked for his money back but stood half a metre away from the purchaser.
2   The experimenter stood close to the purchaser. He was equally

courteous, but as he spoke he lightly held or touched the other person's arm.

The experiment was conducted a number of times over a significant sample of the cigarette-buying population. When money was requested without body contact, the request was refused by 28 per cent of the sample. When body contact was made, the money was returned in every single case. The words used in each situation were identical.

The body signal of touching, coupled with the courteous manner of the experimenter, spoke of friendship. It was a communication that created a relationship of friendship with a stranger. This was a relationship in which a sudden profit – represented by a free packet of cigarettes – was not taken advantage of.

In the sales situation many messages are sent to prospective customers and many are sent out by the customers. To achieve their purpose, not only must all messages be received, but they must also be understood. On the telephone many non-verbal messages are missed. This makes it all the more important that every signal given on the telephone is recognized and understood.

The customer story

Question: When do customers mean what they say?
Answer: Customer statements that are not strictly true fall into two categories:
  1 The customer is deflecting unwanted suppliers.
  2 The customer is preparing to negotiate concessions from the caller.

Getting rid of unwanted suppliers

The skilled and experienced buyer rarely runs down unwanted merchandise that is offered. He or she simply does not buy it:

'Your designs are excellent. I wish I had seen them before. Unfortunately, my budget for the whole year is already spent. Perhaps another time. Goodbye.'

'I am tied up for the next few weeks. Call me at the beginning of the year.'

'Management has put a bar on all buying.'

Given a disarming answer the supplier is disappointed, but not offended. Sometimes, the good-natured customer is positively flattering:

'Your models are the best I have ever seen. If I had not ordered all my stocks, I would certainly have bought from you.'

The caller must take care not to be deceived. Feeling exuberant, because the merchandise or service has been described by the customer on the telephone in glowing terms, does not pay the rent. It is a pitfall to be avoided.

Offers that are rejected – no matter how smoothly – must be treated as objections. The caller probes:

'May I make an appointment now for six weeks time?'

'Would you like a trial delivery on sale or return?'

'May we have an order with invoicing delayed until the next financial period?'

The caller's questions are designed to test the objection to see if it is the major one.

Paving the way to concessions

If a caller is not brushed away by a customer immediately, there is a chance for the caller to reach his or her objective. No buyer claps his or her hands with glee when a caller makes an offer. Many conversations will seem to be low key but there is much in the buyer's armoury to beat down the unwary:

'Greenly Brothers have offered five per cent cash discount.'

'Your competitors have agreed that painting of the machinery in our house colours is included.'

'I have received an offer ten per cent below your price.'

The buyer tells stories or half-truths. The buyer's objective is to secure maximum concessions from the caller against an order that the buyer places. Negotiation is a complex process but anyone can play. There are three basic rules to remember:

1 Never give something for nothing.
2 Never give a concession without trading something in exchange.
3 Always link every concession given to the total contract price. If the buyer is allowed to deal separately with payment, with distribution, with product quality, size, packaging, colour and weight, and with personnel, the sum total of all the concessions gained by the customer will be punitive.

Was something said?

Question: How are listening skills developed?
Answer: Listening skills are improved and developed by employing a technique to neutralize apprehension.

In a telephone conversation the caller has to listen as well as speak. The caller must recognize and react to all the things that he or she hears. Listening is a skill that improves with practice. With the inexperienced, a feeling of apprehension inhibits efficient listening.

Example

Customer 'Yes the winters are very cold in this part of the country. My biggest problem however is that we have been burgled three times this month.'

Representative 'Double glazing will certainly help. With traditional, single skin windows, down draughts are created. It is these that keep the room at a very low temperature. With double glazing a second skin is added to the window which makes the room very warm.'

The prospective customer in this case has needs, of which the most important is security. The inexperienced representative, however, cannot get away from the usual main selling benefits of the double glazing. Much more could be made of the deterrent effect of that second skin of glass. When customer needs are warmth or fuel economy, the benefits of double glazing must be directed to those needs but when the customer needs are different, the benefits must be different. In the example the representative just did not listen to the message that was being communicated of a need for security.

The representative in the example was also apprehensive. He or she desperately wanted to make a sale and was determined to get the sales patter right. But the representative did not listen. Apprehension is experienced as a feeling of tension or nervousness or, sometimes, as sickness in the stomach and the hands sweating.

Apprehension is not confined to telephoning. Tennis players with three match points lose matches. Competition golfers needing a half-metre putt to win lose championships. Apprehension makes the concentration of the caller, and of the sports competitor, slip.

Technique for neutralizing apprehension

There is a technique for overcoming apprehension which is borrowed from Zen philosophy. The following example illustrates the technique: A student violinist, in the north of England, was extremely talented. His gifts were far greater than anyone else's in his class. He practised and he studied and he was talked of as a prodigy. However, whenever he competed in competitions he went to pieces. He should have come first in all the competitions he entered but he never did. One day, before an important competition, his teacher said: 'I will give you the solution to the problem of your nervousness. Forget about the score. Forget about bowing. Forget about timing, Wiggle your toes hard. Concentrate on wiggling your toes.'

The pupil was incredulous but he did as he was told and it worked. He played brilliantly and won the competition.

Provided that a person has the competence to do what he or she is attempting, objectives will be achieved if the inhibiting factors are removed. The competitor, the musician and the sales representative all have the competence to serve, to putt, to play music, and to recognize everything that is heard on the telephone. The excessive concentration on getting it right which builds up tension, is the inhibiting factor. Diverting that concentration to another activity is the key to success.

As the telephone is picked up to make a call, the toes are wiggled furiously. Full attention is given by the caller to the wiggling and concentration must not stop until the call is finished. With each succeeding call, wiggling recommences and concentration on the wiggling activity is resumed.

With the feeling of apprehension neutralized, the skill of listening correctly to the business telephone call can be developed. It is a straightforward process of evaluating everything that is said. Are the customer's statements, questions and comments relevant to the caller's business? If so, how are they to be dealt with?

It is easy for the caller just to hear what he or she wants to hear. Listening correctly makes sure that nothing is overlooked.

Answering questions

Questions: What are the best ways of answering customers' questions?

Answer: Identify the three main categories into which the questions fall. Deal with each category in the standard way.

Customers' questions fall into three major groups:

1 *Information* There is a request for information because:
   (a) The customer has not understood what has been said.
   (b) The customer is near to buying but needs to know something else.
   (c) The customer wants to discuss the product. Many find buying difficult and the final 'Yes' comes only after long agonizing over pros and cons.
   The caller's task when answering questions in this group is straightforward. Benefit statements must be given and the caller needs to recognize whether he or she is near to a sale. In this case it is selling benefit statements that are given. Simple factual information is sufficient when the customer's problem is not understanding or not hearing clearly what has been said by the caller.
2 *Criticism* The customer has a criticism. This arises because the benefits the caller has given to the customer do not fully match the customer needs. Perhaps they do not match at all. The criticism must be treated as an objection to be countered.

Possibly there is a misunderstanding. The task of the caller is to probe and identify the true objection.

Example

Customer 'Did you say eleven pounds fifty per month? That seems a lot.'

Representative 'Yes. It is eleven pounds fifty when the rental contract is only for twelve months. The rates reduce when contract periods are for two, three and five years. What is more, the cost of all service calls is included in that price. Is that your only criticism of the service?'

3 *Smokescreen* The customer gives the first reason thought of to avoid a commitment. If that is countered then there is another objection and another. It is possible that the real objection is never given, despite the caller's attempts to find it out.

The customer sometimes resorts to indignation, anger or abuse and the caller is berated for intruding by telephone into the customer's privacy.

This situation calls for much skill on the part of the caller. It is more difficult to appease someone on the telephone than in a face-to-face situation. The caller's natural charm and winning ways are limited to a narrow communication channel.

The temptation to shrug off the difficult conversation and move on should be resisted. Successes are good. Like landing a very big order, holding a royal flush or picking the hundred to one outsider, winning over difficult customers makes the effort all worthwhile. Starting to have successes on the telephone means that the caller is becoming more effective. The way to successful phoning is effective phoning.

The other point of view

Question: What answers does the customer expect to hear?
Answer: The customer expects to hear the answer that he or she wants to hear.

The caller has good days and bad days. Perhaps the caller needs to make two sales to reach a quota or very much needs to persuade a buyer to keep a delivery that was not quite perfect. Unless there is an established and friendly relationship none of these factors really affect the customer's thinking. The customer's thoughts relate solely to what is important and urgent for the customer.

A customer's profitability is increased by larger discounts; turnover is helped by fast deliveries; outgoing departmental costs are contained if promotional material is provided by manufacturers.

Selling is a process of persuading a buyer to accept the offer and conditions of the seller. The caller is likely to give answers that customers are not expecting to hear. His or her task is to make sure that those answers prove acceptable.

Examples

'And is there a discount on that price?'
'Can you deliver it this afternoon?'
'Are your offices easy to find?'

If the caller gives the right answers to the questions, everything, of course, is fine. When the answers are different, the customer may still accept them. If, however, the customer objects, the caller is equipped to deal with the situation. Objections can be countered and turned to advantage.

Getting the timing right

Question: What is the best time of day to make a call?
Answer: Although the morning is the most expensive time to phone, professional and industrial habits dictate the most effective times.

In the United Kingdom there is a time constraint on telephoning. Charges from 9.00 a.m. to 1.00 p.m. are considerably more expensive than at other times. Behaviour patterns within different industries cut across the charge schedule created by the telephone service.

Examples

Builders reach their offices at 7.30 a.m.
Musicians, who work at night, sleep late in the morning.

Doctors are most easily reached just before and just after morning surgeries.

Telephoning times must be tailored to the habits and needs of the customer. The major constraint is cost. The caller has to judge whether the additional expense is worthwhile. Is waiting until the afternoon a false economy, because the customer is likely to be out and the call will be wasted?

When the caller is new to telephoning in a controlled and skilful way, a few exploratory calls are necessary. They will soon establish the times of the day at which particular types of customers can be contacted. Specific questions must be asked:

'What time of the day is best to call?'
'Please tell me when I am most likely to reach you, during the day?'
'During the day, what time is most convenient for you?'

There are old wives' tales in the world of telephoning such as:

Never telephone a manager before 10.00 a.m. There must be time allowed for dealing with the post.
Before and during lunch is a bad time. After a busy morning the customer thinks of lunch and, more often than not, is not in the mood for doing business.
After 4.30 p.m. is too late because the customer has to deal with his or her own affairs.
There is no point calling a manager before 3.00 p.m. He or she is not back from lunch.

A caller does not really want to start a telephone call at a disadvantage. However, if all the unspoken rules are obeyed, there are about two hours in the morning and one hour in the afternoon in which to telephone.

In practice, there is no ideal time to phone. There is only one rule:

WHEN IT IS NECESSARY TO TELEPHONE – TELEPHONE

If one calls at 6.30 p.m. or 7.00 a.m. or on a Sunday, the worst that can happen is that the receiver is put down. Often, quite a good time to telephone is early morning or late afternoon (when the rates are cheaper). People are fresh first thing in the morning and in the late afternoon they are free of meetings.

When to stop talking

Question: How long should the telephone call be?
Answer: The telephone call should last until the objective is reached. It should then be brought to a close.

In a telephone call time is normally secondary to what has to be said. There are different types of calls. Some need a lot of time while others need little. A call where the objective is a sale needs more time than a call in which an appointment is sought. The selling call itself falls into two separate categories:

1 The prospecting call in which the customer needs have to be identified and benefit messages have to be passed that match those needs. Objections to a sale are likely to arise and must be countered. The caller needs to close the sale with the customer – if it can be done.

2 A supplier offering repeat goods to an existing customer. The conversation here is different. A selling effort is still required because new customer needs may have arisen. There is also the possibility of objections arising as a result of the last delivery of goods or supply of service. Some of the preliminary conversation needed with a prospective customer will not be necessary. With an existing customer, a lot of the necessary basic information will already be on file.

Whatever the type of call the same rule applies:

PLAN WHAT YOU ARE GOING TO SAY AND WHEN THE OBJECTIVE IS REACHED BRING THE CALL TO A CLOSE QUICKLY.

Customer interest wanes when that customer's needs are satisfied and the caller who continues the conversation runs the risk of jeopardizing whatever has been achieved. This is more than ever true when the caller has made a sale. A high proportion of customers – whether the sale is made on the telephone or in a factory or shop – experience post-purchase doubts: Was the decision right? Can the money be better spent elsewhere? The caller who continues talking on the telephone can stimulate fresh objections or put fears into the buyer's mind.

When the objective has been reached, it must be the close for the caller as well as for the customer.

How to get better

Question: How can telephone performance be improved?

Answer: Telephoning skills can be improved by monitoring performance and identifying areas of weakness. Corrective techniques are then adopted.

A tape recorder is required with an inexpensive telephone receiver attachment. If this is not available, a friend or colleague must be prevailed upon and he or she should be asked to monitor a selected number of the conversations. This method is less satisfactory because, unless there are extension telephones, only the caller's part of the call is heard.

The call is analysed against the grid of questions in Figure 5 on page 40. The grid is designed for a sales call to a prospective customer but if the caller wishes to monitor another type of telephone call, only the nature of the objectives needs to be changed.

The objective of the monitoring process itself is to identify weaknesses and strengths in the caller's performance. When they are known the weaknesses can be compensated for. The caller can

CHECKLIST	Yes	No
Did I plan this call in advance ?	☐	☐
Did I make a note of the buyer's name ?	☐	☐
Did I use the buyer's name during the call ?	☐	☐
Did I give my company's name ?	☐	☐
Did I give my name ?	☐	☐
Do you know what the buyer's needs are ?	☐	☐
Did I meet any objections ?	☐	☐
Did I counter the objections effectively ?	☐	☐
Did I offer benefits to match the customer's specific needs ?	☐	☐
Did I ask for an order ?	☐	☐
Did I ask for an appointment ?	☐	☐
If I failed, did I leave an opening for another call ?	☐	☐

Figure 8   *Checklist for performance evaluation*

build on his or her own observed strengths by making them even better still.

Another form of performance evaluation is the DIY checklist as shown in Figure 8.

Read through the checklist ticking the appropriate boxes. If there are any 'No s', list below the corrective action to be taken.

At first the checklist should be used after every call. Once the caller reaches a satisfactory level of competence in telephoning, the assessment checklist should be used once a fortnight and then once a month. It is always a good idea to check to make sure that no bad habits have developed. If mistakes are not recognized they will tend to be repeated. Every repetition is a reinforcement of something wrong and the caller may find that he or she is succeeding less often without knowing the reason why.

Getting communication right

Question: How can the communication process be improved?
Answer: Monitor conversations to see where communication falls below an acceptable standard. Take steps to remedy problems by improving the use of language.

If an order is required from a buyer and it is obtained as a result of a telephone call, is the communication process adequate? Similarly, if an appointment is obtained, a complaining customer satisfied or a person asking questions provided with acceptable information, is the communication level satisfactory?

It is always possible to get better, even by the smallest margin. One remembers the years of effort needed by athletes to run a measured mile in four minutes. The record was always out of reach but one day Dr Roger Bannister achieved the impossible and the current running record stands at nearly ten seconds less than that time.

The need to improve communication becomes most urgent when objectives are not reached. Orders that slip away or appointments that are not granted are evidence of inadequacy in some way and poor communication may be one of the weaknesses. The checklist in Figure 9 analyses the level of communication in a conversation.

Read through the checklist and tick the appropriate boxes. If the answer to any question is 'No', write below the reasons for that answer.

Often the most likely reason for a 'No' answer is language. Simple, uncomplicated language is most effective. Short sentences should be used. A pause is often as effective as a stream of words. Where there is indication of a problem the words that were used should be written down. The written word makes evaluation easier.

Examples

'. . . and the Pine range is particularly good value because not only was it voted Kitchen Furniture of the Year, which it wouldn't have been if it hadn't been such good value, not only for this year, but also for the past five years, but since the price, compared with other similar types of furniture, and you know for the past ten years the company policy has been to give the most competitive price level in the market . . .'

There is another way of saying the same thing using short sentences:

CHECKLIST	Yes	No
Does the person spoken to understand exactly what is said ?	☐	☐
Does the caller clearly understand the replies ?	☐	☐
Are appropriate answers given to questions asked by the caller ?	☐	☐
Are appropriate answers given to questions asked by the customer ?	☐	☐
Does the customer recognize benefit messages as such ?	☐	☐
Does the caller recognize needs described by the customer ?	☐	☐
Does the caller recognize needs that are not described by the customer ?	☐	☐
Does either party have to ask for something to be repeated ?	☐	☐
Did the customer sound puzzled/angry/worried ?	☐	☐
Was the conversation completed without the customer asking for something to be repeated ?	☐	☐

Figure 9 *Checklist for evaluating the level of communication*

'. . . and the Pine range is particularly good value. It was voted Kitchen Furniture of the Year. It has carried the vote for the past five years. The price gives wonderful value compared with the price of similar furniture.

'It has been company policy for the past ten years to give the most competitive price level in the market. The Pine range is a bargain that must not be missed. . . .'

Short clear sentences communicate best.

Summary

Questions	Answers
1 What is meant by communication?	In simple terms communication is the process of passing and receiving messages.
2 When do customers mean what they say?	Customer statements that are not strictly true fall into two categories: 1 The customer is deflecting unwanted suppliers. 2 The customer is preparing to negotiate concessions from the caller.
3 How are listening skills developed?	Listening skills are improved and developed by employing a technique to neutralize apprehension.
4 What are the best ways of answering customers' questions?	Identify the three main categories into which the questions fall. Deal with each category in the standard way.
5 What answers does the customer expect to hear?	The customer expects to hear the answer that he or she wants to hear.
6 What is the best time of day to make a call?	Although morning is the most expensive time to phone, professional and industrial habits dictate the most effective times.
7 How long should the telephone call be?	The telephone call should last until the objective is reached. It should then be brought to a close.
8 How can telephone performance be improved?	Telephoning skills can be improved by monitoring performance and identifying areas of weakness. Corrective techniques are then adopted.

9 How can the communication process be improved?

Monitor conversations to see where communication falls below an acceptable standard. Take steps to remedy problems by improving the use of language.

How to plan the sales call

As with previous chapters, answer the questions set out below before proceeding. The answers are collected in a summary at the end of the chapter.

Questions

1 What is the best way to turn a quotation into an order?
2 Are sales calls wasted after deliveries have been despatched?
3 What is the best way to rescue a cancelled order?
4 What is the best way to get repeat business?
5 Which customers shall I call today?
6 What is the most effective arrangement of calls during the day?
7 What is the best way of re-establishing contact with previous purchasers?

Answers

Chapter 6   How to plan the sales call

Clinching the order – What happens afterwards? – Salvage operations – Getting repeat business – Whose turn is it? – Getting the timing right – Reviving dormant contacts – Summary

Clinching the order

Question: What is the best way to turn a quotation into an order?
Answer: Speak to the buyer a few days later, and sell.

Whether initial contact is by letter, phone or visit, every quotation made must always be confirmed in writing.

Rule 1:   Allow the buyer time to consider. A quotation is made in circumstances where an order is not closed on the spot. Unless there is an indication that contact with the buyer should follow immediately after the quotation is sent, five working days is a convenient time to wait.

Rule 2:   Follow up the quotation and push for a sale. Some buyers are willing to buy but instead they do nothing. There are three main reasons:

    (a)   Inertia.
    (b)   Pressure of work.
    (c)   The buyer wants to negotiate better terms. If he or she waits until they are contacted, instead of being the first to open discussion, the buyer is in a stronger position.

Care must be taken when fresh contact with the buyer is made. Words must be carefully chosen. It is important to avoid a direct rebuff.

Example

'Hello, Mr Edwards. This is Brian Howard of Brentwood Refrigeration Ltd. We sent you a quotation last week for industrial freezer capsules. Have you had an opportunity to arrive at a decision?'

If Mr Edwards is asked, instead:

'. . . we sent you a quotation last week. Will you buy?'

there is the possibility of a direct 'No'. This is more difficult to deal with than a 'No' to the question of whether there was time to look at the quotation. If the caller suspects there is any doubt that the order will be placed, there is an immediate opportunity to add selling benefit messages to sway the decision.

What happens afterwards?

Question: Are sales calls wasted after deliveries have been despatched?

Answer: Sales calls are never wasted. Depending on the industry, the follow-up call generates further business or contributes to sound PR.

Fast moving, low-priced goods are not in the selling outlet long and there is frequent contact between seller and buyer. The function of asking whether the delivery is satisfactory to the buyer is combined with the activity of taking a fresh order:

'Good morning Mr James. I trust sales are buoyant. We despatched order 7078 last week. Will you be keeping to the same size range next time?'

When the unit price of a product or service is high, rather than low, there is often a much longer interval between buyer/seller contacts. With some products or services – for example, industrial machinery, factory premises, exterior stone cleaning – the possibility of repeat business is remote indeed. Although the buyer needs are satisfied by the single purchase, it is good selling practice for the supplier to make a follow-up call to ensure that everything is in order.

Businesses grow. Market demands change. Consumer attitudes to product acceptance change. There are also changes in fashion and in technology. The process of business is a dynamic process and because of this it is always necessary to keep an eye on the future. Customer loyalty is frequently based on convenience and loyalty bonds are reinforced by a supplier's efficiency and reliability. Efficiency means making sure that deliveries are on time and that they are correct. Reliability means making sure, over and over again, that deliveries are correct and on time. Making sure that everything is happening according to plan reinforces the bond of customer loyalty. It does not take long to do and it is not difficult. All that is required is a telephone call to ensure that everything is as it should be:

'Hello, Mr Edwards. It is Brian Howard calling, of Brentwood Refrigeration Ltd. I am just making sure that the delivery to you last week took place as planned. I am not expecting to hear of problems, but our policy is alway to double-check. So everything is okay, I trust.'

Salvage operations

Question: What is the best way to rescue a cancelled order?
Answer: Identify, if possible, the real reason for the cancellation. Sell.

Cancelled orders are always unpleasant. There are three major reasons for a buyer to cancel an order:
1 The buyer has received a better offer from elsewhere. It is unlikely that the buyer will disclose this. If it is in fact the case, the situation is well nigh impossible to retrieve.
2 There is a routine company policy that stipulates automatic cancellation if all requirements of the printed company order are not explicitly fulfilled. For this situation a sales call is essential.
  Buyers are flexible. If there is the same value to the buyer in having the delivery as there was when the order was placed, it should be possible to have the cancellation lifted. It is wise to

110

precede the sales benefits with a degree of humility and repentance that matches the misdeed:

'Hello, Mr Edwards. This is Brian Howard of Brentwood Refrigeration Ltd. I am calling about the order for industrial freezer capsules. It is your order number 78214. The goods were delivered to your Essex factory, as instructed, but they were refused on arrival. I am terribly sorry, Mr Edwards. I know that, for exceptional reasons to do with our production line, the goods were one day late. This inexcusable inefficiency is quite alien to our company practice. We really do supply industry with a large volume of our freezer capsules. Do you remember, when we discussed the product, the savings they could help you achieve. This won't change. May we redeliver?'

3   Bad communication between seller and buyer. Conditions laid down in the buyer's order have not apparently been fulfilled, or the circumstances are beyond the supplier's control or the supplier has made no attempt to advise and inform the buyer:

'Hello, Mr Edwards. Brian Howard of Brentwood Refrigeration Ltd. I have received your cancellation for the order for industrial freezer capsules, order number 78214. I am sorry for this delay. I know you wanted the goods in September and it is now October. The order stipulated delivery in the UK in September. In fact the goods arrived at Southampton on August 30th from our parent plant in Michigan and they have been delayed all this time by the dock strike. We received the capsules yesterday and they are in the process of being adapted to your specification. We should have advised you and I am afraid we did not. I do apologize. Mr Edwards, the capsules will still help you to achieve the savings we discussed. May we deliver tomorrow?'

Getting repeat business

Question: What is the best way to get repeat business?
Answer: Sell the product benefits continuously to the buyer, even though the goods are ordered regularly.

With some types of product business is regular between buyer and seller. The problem for the buyer is not whether or not to buy the product, it is with whom to place the order. Once a relationship is established, orders are given continuously. This relationship is sustained until something occurs to disrupt it.

Example A fresh pizza manufacturer telephones delicatessen customers regularly on, say, Monday and Wednesday mornings to take down order details. The size and nature of the order varies slightly, depending on how long the shop's customers take to buy up the stocks. The temptation to relegate the order taking to a non-sales person must be strongly resisted. Even when the buyer knows his or her job thoroughly, there are realistic opportunities to increase order sizes:

> 'Thank you, Miss Rudolph. I will see that the eleven dozen pizzas are sent out this afternoon with Robin's delivery. By the way, is the abattoir strike affecting your deliveries of meat pies and sausage rolls? Would your customers like to take our salami pizzas, if they cannot buy your usual pies?'

Not all repeat business is given promptly. Sales may be seasonal. In other situations repeat business is a result of the last purchase being sold. Outside of the low-priced, fast-moving consumer goods scene, getting repeat business lacks the comforting label of 'regular'. The caller has to be ready to sell rather than just to take down details. It is therefore necessary to combine the question asking whether the delivered goods have been sold with sales benefits:

> 'Hello, Mr Edwards. This is Brian Howard of Brentwood Refrigeration Ltd. I hope all your customers now have profitable extra efficiency from your equipment using our capsules. Is your success with them continuing?'

One of the most effective methods of closing an initial order is to ask for it directly:

> 'Will you buy it?'
> 'Do you want one?'

Many people do not use this technique because, although it is effective, they are apprehensive. A direct 'No' prejudices the presentation and it may kill the sale.

In the context of trying to obtain repeat business, the direct question 'Will you buy another?' is not recommended as an early question. The direct close in the classical sales situation follows after the process of customer qualification, objection handling and the passing of benefit messages to fit customer needs. When trying for repeat business, some of the information arising from the first sales situation is forgotten. The caller knows that an order was placed but he or she forgets what the real reasons are.

Asking for repeat business involves selling the benefits of that business, tailored to the real needs of the customer, at the same time.

Whose turn is it?

Question: Which customers shall I call today?
Answer: There must be a calling rota, so that all customer categories are covered in the most productive way.

In many industries much of the business that is obtained comes from a relatively small number of customers. In the nineteenth century, Pareto, an economist, propounded a theory on the subject which stated that in most situations 80 per cent of the total results could be attributed to 20 per cent of the total activity. For example, an airline currently finds that 20 per cent of its routes generate 80 per cent of its revenue. Similarly, a food company discovers that about 80 per cent of its orders come from 20 per cent of its sales representatives.

A profile of a company's customers shows which groups give the most business. Sales calls to customers must concentrate heavily on those from whom good business is certain to come. The smaller customers must not be dropped. They must be contacted regularly, at a frequency of once for every two, three or four calls made to the more important clients.

There is no fixed rule about who to call. If business policy is to have a spread of different industry customers, rather than specializing in one particular industry, a pattern of calling must be planned.

Example A caller prospecting for new business for a bakery. The five or six major groups of new customers with which the bakery does business are identified – sales records give the information required. The breakdown of orders shows:

50 per cent of orders from catering contractors
30 per cent of orders from hotels
6 per cent of orders from British Rail
14 per cent of orders from miscellaneous sources

To maintain the balance, calls should be made in approximately the same ratio:

Catering contractors	Hotels	British Rail	Other
10	3	1	3

Getting the timing right

Question: What is the most effective arrangement of calls during the day?

Answer: Efficiency results from careful planning of calls, in respect of sequence and time to be taken.

Making the most effective use of time is the result of planning. Efficiency follows from careful planning.

What are the activities leading up to the reading of this page?

Has time been wasted?
Have time and energy been allocated so that the greatest part has been spent on the most important tasks?
Have all the tasks originally planned been done?

Days fill up easily with things to do. Sometimes when there is the least business to do, more and more inconsequential tasks appear.

Rules for managing personal time effectively

Rule 1: Analyse the objectives to be achieved. To do this, take a sheet of paper. Enter a column heading 'Objectives'. Underneath write down all that is to be achieved in the following week.

114

Example Tom Grammond – new car salesman. What are the activities that must be carried out in the week?

Objectives

1 Check discrepancy in commission statement with accounts department.
2 Take prospective customer Smith and prospective customer Leadbetter for demonstration drives. Appointments are already arranged for Tuesday and Thursday.
3 Have daily morning sales meeting with sales manager and other salesmen.
4 Write out daily reports of activities.
5 Make telephone call backs to prospective customers Getty, Hendry, Filpot, Sayner, Jennings and Gardwood. Initial contacts made in previous two weeks.
6 Make five prospecting telephone calls per day.
7 Arrange for total of twenty prospecting letters to be sent out in the week.
8 Follow up by telephone eight outstanding prospecting letters from last week.
9 See the printer to confirm layout of promotional material for distribution at tennis club.
10 Be present at delivery of new cars to customers Kelly and Colne.
11 Deal with average of four prospective customers daily who walk into showroom.

Rule 2: Place items in order of priority. In some cases the items all seem to be of equal importance. The 8.30 a.m. meeting is company policy. Only a good reason can change it. Demonstration appointments already arranged with prospective customers are important. Call backs on the telephone to prospective customers at promised times must be kept. With regard to the deliveries of new cars, Mr Kelly is talking about a second car for his daughter. He would be offended if Tom Grammond were not present and it might jeopardize the second order. Being present at the delivery of the new car to Mr Colne is desirable but it is not quite so important. Prospecting calls are important, but they are flexible.

In the following list the objectives 1 to 11 have been arranged in order of priority. The essential activities are at the head of the column and the remaining tasks follow in order of importance.

3   Have daily morning sales meeting.
2   Take Mr Smith and Mr Leadbetter for demonstration drives.
4   Write out daily reports of activities.
10 Be present at delivery of new cars to Mr Kelly and Mr Colne.
5   Make telephone call backs to customers Getty, Hendry, Filpot Sayner, Jennings and Gardwood.
11 Deal with average of four prospective customers daily who walk into showroom.
6   Make five prospecting calls per day.
8   Follow up by telephone eight outstanding letters from last week.
7   Arrange for total of twenty prospecting letters to be sent out in the week.
9   See printer to confirm layout of promotional material for distribution at tennis club.
1   Check discrepancy in commission statement with accounts department.

Rule 3:   Allocate time to be spent on each activity. If a disproportionate emphasis is permitted, it will diminish the productivity of the total day.

Rule 4:   After events have taken place, record actual times taken. Compare actual and assessed times. Modify future activities in the light of what performance revealed.

One day – Tuesday – has been taken out of Tom Grammond's programme for the week to illustrate what happened. The estimated and actual time for the tasks are shown as follows:

Tuesday		*Hours*	
		Estimated time	*Actual time*
8.30– 9.00	Sales meeting	½	½
9.00–10.00	Prospecting calls/ showroom	1	1
10.00–11.00	Printers to approve material	1	2¼
11.00–12.15	Demonstration appointment – Smith	1¼	late/ cancelled
12.15– 1.00	Prospecting calls/ showroom	¾	¾

Tuesday		Hours	
		Estimated time	Actual time
14.00–15.00	Demonstration appointment – Blake (arranged Monday)	1¼	2
15.00–15.30	Delivery of car to Kelly	½	missed
15.30–15.45	Appointment with accounts department to check commission statement	¼	¼
15.45–17.00	Prospecting calls/ showroom	1¼	1¼
17.00	Complete daily report		
17.00–18.00	Prospecting calls/ showroom	1	1

Comparison of the two time columns shows the discrepancies that have occurred. The journey to the printers and the time spent there took twice as long as expected. This resulted in a cancelled demonstration appointment. The prospective customer was justifiably angry that the salesman was not there. After waiting fifteen minutes he cancelled the appointment. Unfortunately, there was no other salesperson available to help at the time and the potential sale was lost.

The demonstration in the afternoon, arranged the day before, also took longer than expected, but it resulted in a sale. It was unfortunate that Tom Grammond was not present at the appointed time for delivery of the new motor car to his client. However, he resolved the situation by making a point of telephoning Mr Kelly to explain why he was not there thereby demonstrating his genuine interest and concern that all was in order for his customer.

With hindsight, the journey to the printers was not one that Tom Grammond could achieve quickly. The roads he had to travel on are always busy with traffic. If work days are planned regularly, mistakes of this nature are not often repeated because realistic times for tasks are allocated.

Analysis of tasks and times taken sometimes gives an unexpected perspective of sales activities. Perhaps too much is being attempted or the sales territory is too big. Are too many customers being serviced? Are new business targets unrealistic?

Efficient planning is the way to approach these questions. Management and sales personnel must find the answers.

Reviving dormant contacts

Question: What is the best way of re-establishing contact with previous purchasers?

Answer: A selling call is the best way of re-establishing a lost contact, coupled with specific benefit messages relating to known areas of contention.

When business is strong there is an active relationship between supplier and buyer. There are regular meetings and many telephone calls. Gradually, however, a change creeps in. Sales drop because there are one or two inadequate deliveries – colours are wrong – sizes are muddled – service is defective – quantities are inaccurate. The friendly relationship changes and a one-time major client becomes just a ledger entry.

After a time, the former working relationship with such clients can be picked up again. Personnel in companies change. Trading patterns change. The call that must be made, however, is not another selling call as for a new customer or for repeat business. There must be extra selling benefits. The specific reasons why business is no longer placed will be known by the old customer. Even if personnel have changed, reputations linger. The call is carefully planned. Normal product or service benefit statements must be passed and selling benefits to pre-empt discussion of old problems must be included early on.

Example
'Mr Knight, my name is Simpkins of Simpkins Labels Ltd. We are old suppliers of labels to your company. We have just had a spring-clean. We have changed our equipment to a fully automated production line. This is why I am calling. In most cases we can now offer a two day service. Our prices are rock bottom. May I call and show you some new designs?'

Summary

Questions	Answers
1 What is the best way to turn a quotation into an order?	Speak to the buyer a few days later, and sell.
2 Are sales calls wasted after deliveries have been despatched?	Sales calls are never wasted. Depending on the industry, the follow-up call generates further business or contributes to sound PR.
3 What is the best way to rescue a cancelled order?	Identify, if possible, the real reason for the cancellation. Sell.
4 What is the best way to get repeat business?	Sell the product benefits continuously to the buyer, even though the goods are ordered regularly.
5 Which customers shall I call today?	There must be a calling rota, so that all customer categories are covered in the most productive way.
6 What is the most effective arrangement of calls during the day?	Efficiency results from careful planning of calls, in respect of sequence and time to be taken.
7 What is the best way of re-establishing contact with previous purchasers?	A selling call is the best way of re-establishing a lost contact, coupled with specific benefit messages relating to known areas of contention.

Chapter 7

How to plan the sales presentation

The first section of this chapter deals with the pre-planning stage. The questions below are concerned with that preliminary phase. Please answer the questions – the answers are to be found on the next page. The test has been set to provide a framework for the contents of the second section.

Section 1   Pre-planning stage

Questions   **Answers**

1 When does the presentation begin?

2 Is it true that a sale is made or lost in the first few seconds of contact?

3 What are the objectives of a presentation?

4 What action is required from a buyer?

5 What sorts of thing would a buyer say to suggest that an order is possible?

6 What types of question should the buyer be asked?

7 What kinds of answer is a buyer likely to give?

8 What kinds of question is a buyer likely to ask?

Questions

9 What kinds of benefit message should be offered?

10 Are there any other types of benefit that would contribute to securing an order?

11 What actions are necessary if an order is placed by a buyer?

12 Is there anything that might make a buyer reverse a decision to buy?

13 What actions are necessary if an order is not given?

14 In what ways should an order be asked for?

15 What types of information should be known about product deliveries?

16 How long is a presentation likely to take?

Answers

Section 1 Pre-planning stage

Questions

Answers

1 When does the presentation begin?

The presentation begins right back at the pre-planning stage. The caller is at a definite disadvantage if he or she makes it all up on the spur of the moment.

2 Is it true that a sale is made or lost in the first few seconds of contact?

All parts of the presentation are important. But it is certainly true that a sale is not possible unless the customer's total attention is secured.

3 What are the objectives of a presentation?

There are many objectives – a trial order – a repeat order – a contract for regular deliveries – part repeat business and part new business. The objective is related to the industry, and the caller's needs.

4 What action is required from a buyer? .

Encouragement from the buyer, if it is given, is very welcome. If an order materializes then a special order number is usually necessary. For a first time order it is important that the caller receives an official order on the customer's headed notepaper.

5 What sorts of thing would a buyer say to suggest that an order is possible?

A good buyer wants to be certain of reliability of delivery dates and quality control and is concerned that suppliers deliver precisely as specified. Comments or questions on this aspect of business are not unusual.

6 What types of question should the buyer be asked?

The caller must quickly identify precise needs – urgency of delivery – volume of potential business – possible size of an immediate order – number of

	competitors – purchase price levels, if they exist – packaging requirements. In many cases a caller strikes a deal only after relevant customer information is obtained during the presentation. The questions necessary to secure that information are carefully worked out during the early planning stage.
7 What kinds of answer is a buyer likely to give?	As a general rule buyers are no less or no more unethical than sellers. Many of the answers given to questions are factual but the caller must judge whether a few critical answers have been slightly exaggerated to secure a better price or better conditions.
8 What kinds of question is a buyer likely to ask?	With a prospective supplier, a buyer must be sure of the credibility of that supplier. He or she must make sure that there is the capacity to meet all the demands of an order. The following are likely questions: Which other clients are supplied? How big is the factory or warehouse? What volume of stocks is carried? What is the normal lead time for execution of orders? What are the normal arrangements in respect of raw materials?
9 What kinds of benefit message should be offered?	There are two major kinds of benefit message:

Questions	Answers
	1 Product knowledge statements.
	2 Selling benefit messages.
	They must all be listed before the presentation.
10 Are there any other types of benefit that would contribute to securing an order?	The list should be as comprehensive as possible – short-term benefits – long-term export market benefits. Everything must be considered in case it is needed in the presentation.
11 What actions are necessary if an order is placed by a buyer?	The caller must ensure that payment terms are agreed and confirmed. If appropriate, stocks or production capacity must be reserved.
12 Is there anything that might make a buyer reverse a decision to buy?	Once the caller has achieved his or her objective, the presentation must be brought to a close quickly. Continuous light discussion runs the risk of generating fresh objections that may be difficult to overcome.
13 What actions are necessary if an order is not given?	The buyer's refusal must be treated as an objection. The caller has to identify any other objections that have not been disclosed. The caller must not give up.
14 In what ways should an order be asked for?	The most effective way to get an order is to ask for it. There are a number of other closes – the assumptive close, the alternatives close, the last one close and the lock close – but none are as effective as asking directly.
15 What types of information should be known about product deliveries?	The caller must know every piece of information that would be specified in an order. The major aspects are: price, weight,

Questions	Answers

Answers

packaging, guarantee periods, part replacement'facilities, service back-up, training requirements.

16 How long is a presentation likely to take?

If the presentation has the objective of selling a product or service, it must not be hurried. If the objective is to take an order then the problem is simplified. Facts are simply stated and an order is then placed. The presentation to sell, however, must qualify needs, establish the caller's credibility, pass benefit statements and counteract all objections. At the end of the presentation the close leads to the order.

Chapter 7

How to plan the sales presentation

Section 2

Answer the following questions before reading this section. The answers are collected together in a summary at the end of this chapter.

Questions	Answers
1 How is the problem of reaching the buyer overcome?	
2 What are the main types of presentation?	
3 How does a buyer think?	
4 What makes buyers buy?	

Chapter 7 How to plan the sales presentation

Section 2

Getting through – The routes to the sale – The buyer's point of view – Buyer motivation – Summary

The sales presentation on the telephone is of paramount importance. It either has the objective of a sale or, in some cases, it is the forerunner of a face-to-face meeting that leads to a sale.

Consumer goods

The sales presentation for consumer goods closes for the objective without delay. Consumer goods are those that are used or consumed by the purchaser. The buyer's problems are:

Which goods to buy?
What price level?
What stocking level to adopt?
How many competing lines?

Industrial goods

The sales presentation for industrial goods does not close immediately. The reason is that in the majority of situations, the buyer does not yet know precisely what is wanted. There are a number of differences between consumer and industrial goods:

Industrial goods are used by the purchaser to produce an end product.
The industrial sale is a 'one off'.
The unit cost is substantially higher.
Industrial goods have a high technology component.
The buyer is usually not one person but a committee of specialists.

The industrial sale is a series of problem-solving exercises to define the customer's real problem and evolve an effective solution. The objective of the sales presentation with industrial goods, therefore, is to sell the credibility and capability of the caller and his or her company.

Getting through

Question: How is the problem of reaching the buyer overcome?
Answer: Making contact with a buyer is only a problem if the caller thinks of it as such. Making contact is a matter of giving short, polite instructions to whoever is encountered on the telephone.

There are three main situations in which the caller telephones to make a presentation:

1   The buyer has given an invitation:

'I am too busy to speak to you now. Ring me tomorrow morning and tell me about your merchandise.'

2   There has been previous contact or business with the buyer. The caller knows that when he or she makes contact there is going to be an opportunity to make a presentation.
3   The caller is prospecting for business with new customers. In this situation every call is a presentation. The approach to use is covered in Chapter 1.

Getting through needs only a firm authoritative manner. The instructions are short and business-like:

'Please put me through to Mrs Green, the haberdashery buyer. This is Mr Shield of Silken Trimmings Ltd.'

The routes to the sale

Question: What are the main types of presentation?
Answer: There are three major types:
1 The scripted presentation.
2 The AIDA plan.
3 The need fulfilment presentation.

Management policy in a company frequently dictates the type of presentation adopted by its sales force.

The scripted presentation

There are many advantages to this approach. Newcomers are required to learn a set script which means that the hard work of cutting their teeth in the field is bypassed. The script should be prepared by an experienced salesperson.

The objective of the scripted presentation is to secure a sale or to secure a demonstration appointment and the objective does not vary. It is in these circumstances that the script is so successful. Without the buyer knowing it the presentation becomes routine for the caller. The caller's voice projects enthusiasm and authority but the hard work has been taken out. The operating rules for preparing the script are given in Chapter 1.

The AIDA plan

A   Attention
I   Interest
D   Desire
A   Action

The objectives are to sell the caller's products rather than to satisfy specific customer needs. There is, of course, an overlap. When a customer is found not to have needs that the caller's products satisfy, the caller moves on. AIDA is a sales exercise – it is not a marketing activity. There are four steps:

Attention

First the caller has to gain the attention of the customer. This is achieved by a combination of the caller's manner and words that command immediate attention:

'I have been recommended by Mr Jones.'
'The managing director asked me to speak to you.'
'I am told that you speak French fluently.'

Interest

Interest is generated by the caller referring to a benefit which satisfies one or more of the customer's needs:

'We make reusable seals.'
'Our prices are the cheapest.'
'We carry stocks.'

Desire

The caller generates desire by showing how he or she is able to provide the benefits and how, if the customer does nothing about securing them, they will be lost.

Additionally, desire is created by offering subsidiary benefits such as savings through special discounts or bulk purchase, or the advantage of privileged ownership. It is made clear to the buyer that if nothing is done the benefits will go to competitors or will not be available later.

Action

Action is a form of closing. To achieve the promised benefits, the buyer must send a telex, write out an order, or send a deposit. Whatever is necessary for the sale contract to be established must be carried out.

Example A representative wishes to sell a children's encyclopaedia to a prospective customer. The customer is the parent of four schoolchildren.

In order to prepare for the presentation take a sheet of paper. Write the four headings of AIDA across the page and underneath each heading write all the comments and offers that should be made. This is illustrated in Figure 10.

When the planning is completed, the caller is ready to telephone and make the presentation. AIDA is a structure which forms the bones of the presentation. It is up to the caller to fill it out with his or her own words.

Attention	Interest	Desire	Action
Greet customer by name	Help in passing exams	Hire purchase benefits	Offer free trial period
Recommended by a named friend	Most up to date source of knowledge	Massive discount for paperback edition	Invite children to use books
Has been directed by school	Acclaimed by critics for literary achievement	Children will not fall behind	Ask for commitment
I hear you have four clever children	Short-cut research facilities	Achievement of other children who have bought publication	Offer to demonstrate help from books for current homework

Figure 10   *The AIDA plan*

The need fulfilment presentation

The need fulfilment presentation makes use of aspects of both the AIDA plan and the scripted presentation but it is a more flexible type of presentation. From within the resources of his or her company the caller wants to satisfy the needs and wants of the customer and take an order. At the beginning of the call the caller frequently has no more than a hunch as to what is required. The sequence of steps is as follows:

Introduction
Qualification of customer needs
Selection of appropriate product or service
Passing of benefit messages
Handling objections
Closing

Example

    Caller 'Hello, Mr Barrett. This is the Apex Engineering Company. Wilson speaking. I met your sales director yesterday and he suggested that I make myself known to you.'

    Customer 'Oh yes. There are no immediate problems that I cannot cope with in the factory. What is it that you do?'

    Caller 'We have opened a factory on the next estate. We have a turning shop and a paint shop. We do a lot of plate welding and we also have capacity for jobbing engineering. Is there any way we could help you?'

    Customer 'Well, our ventilation system is not as efficient as it might be.'

The buyer's point of view

Question: How does a buyer think?

Answer: Buyers are concerned with improving the profitability of their organization or department. Other considerations are secondary to that interest.

With consumer goods and with most service activities directed towards the public, a buyer is appointed because of his or her qualities of judgement, experience and administrative skill. A high level of numeracy is of value and flair is important. Where fashion is concerned, artistic and colour sense count too. The buyer's function is to find and buy goods which the company is able to sell at a profit.

Unless the buying function is newly created, sources of supply are inherited by the buyer. Divisional or departmental targets are set by management for the buyer to achieve. The buyer may, or may not, participate in the setting of these targets but, once formulated, the targets must be reached.

Each year there is a drive to reach higher turnover and higher profitability, so the targets get bigger.

It is useful for the person selling on the telephone to stop and think frequently: 'How will the buyer react to this?' or 'What else does the buyer have to think of other than price and quantity?'.

Buyers are concerned with problems of storage and with labelling and packaging. They need to generate maximum return for every square metre of storage space. Within a retail store buyers jostle for prime display positions.

Thinking of a company's products from the buyer's point of view throws up buyer needs. The caller can offer appropriate benefits without waiting for the buyer to spell out specific needs:

'Our products can be stacked, one on top of the other. The different colours combine with dramatic effect. This means that using very little space, you can make an effective display of the whole range.'

Buyer motivation

Question: What makes buyers buy?
Answer: Buyers as consumers buy to satisfy their own needs. Company buyers buy for two major reasons:
1 To satisfy the known demands of their customers.
2 To attract new customers by offering new merchandise that will stimulate them to buy.

When the individual buys a car, or a home extension, or a freezer unit, he or she is satisfying a major need. But the process is more complex than that because many social, economic and psychological pressures are at work:

Is it better than the Jones's?
Is it respectable?
Does it make me look important?
What will the neighbours think?
Is it a wise investment?

The caller who understands the buyer's motivation is in a better position to close his or her sale.

Company buyers have their bread and butter needs. There is a regular type of merchandise that sells and, within limits, the buyer's selection of this type of goods is straightforward. However, buyers also have requirements for something innovative. For this reason, in theory, buyers should be receptive to a new supplier with something fresh to offer. However, in practice, day-to-day matters create pressures and buyers put up barriers to new suppliers.

A supplier wanting to show a range to a new buyer should state what is wanted in a direct manner:

> 'Hello, Mrs Jilds. This is Tom Brainin of Featherstone Furnishings Ltd. You don't know us, but we manufacture lounge and dining-room furnishing fabrics. May I show you our autumn range? It is in the medium-ranged price bracket.'

The buyer may not buy because it is one of those days when everything goes wrong. If the reason given is that the buying budget is exhausted, then the caller must push to show his or her goods nevertheless. A non-productive first call may be an investment for the next season. Buyers remember merchandise.

A good buyer knows everything that is going on in his or her field. Buyers go to trade fairs and they read the trade press because it is their business to know the important suppliers.

If a supplier does business with important national customers, this should be made a selling point:

> 'Hello, Mrs Jilds. This is Tom Brainin of Featherstone Furnishings Ltd. You don't know us but we manufacture lounge and dining-room furnishing fabrics. We supply G Plan and Ercol. May I show you our autumn range?'

Summary

Questions	*Answers*
1 How is the problem of reaching the buyer overcome?	Making contact with a buyer is only a problem if the caller thinks of it as such. Making contact is a matter of giving short, polite instructions to whoever is encountered on the telephone.
2 What are the main types of presentation?	There are three major types: 1 The scripted presentation. 2 The AIDA plan. 3 The need fulfilment presentation.
3 How does a buyer think?	Buyers are concerned with improving the profitability of their organization or department. Other considerations are secondary to that interest.
4 What makes buyers buy?	Buyers as consumers buy to satisfy their own needs. Company buyers buy for two major reasons: 1 To satisfy the known demands of their customers. 2 To attract new customers by offering new merchandise that will stimulate them to buy.

Chapter 8

How to close that sale

Answer the following questions before reading the chapter. The answers are collected together in a summary at the end of this chapter.

Questions	Answers
1 What is a trial close?	
2 What is a buying signal?	
3 What kinds of obstacle are met in closing a sale?	
4 What is the best way to close?	
5 What is the best time to close?	
6 What should be done if the close is not successful?	

Chapter 8   How to close that sale

Testing the water – Obstacles – Closing – Timing – Not giving up –
Summary

Testing the water

Question: What is a trial close?
Answer: A trial close is a technique for testing the progress
         towards a sale achieved in a presentation.

In a sales presentation there are a number of methods of closing.
Some are good – some are brilliant. The type of close employed
often reflects the personality and attitudes of the person who uses
it. The caller has to make a judgement as to when it is right to close
and he or she is helped towards this by buying signals.

Question: What is a buying signal?
Answer: A buying signal is an indication given by the customer –
         by manner or by what is said – that he or she is very
         interested in what is being offered.

   Buying signals are given to a caller in three ways:

1   As answers to trial close questions:
      Caller   'Do you think it is easy to handle?'
      Customer   'Yes. It does seem simple.'
      Caller   'Do you like it in black?'
      Customer   'Yes. It is right for my complexion.'

2   In the form of questions asked by the customer:

      'If I buy one, how long will it take to deliver?'

'What after sales service does it carry?'
'Does your company offer hire purchase terms?'

3   By non-verbal signals given spontaneously by the customer. On the telephone the customer perhaps chuckles, relaxes in mood and becomes less aggressive and more enthusiastic. The customer in the face-to-face situation perhaps smiles, becomes more animated and moves closer to the seller.

The first way in which buying signals are given – that is, as answers to trial close questions – is the most important because trial close questions are in the control of the caller. A positive answer to a trial close question is a buying signal.

The trial close leads up to the real close. It seeks a commitment from the prospective customer, but not yet on the major issue of whether the customer will buy or not buy. There is advantage to be gained from using trial close questions continuously throughout the sales presentation. The close is not something that happens suddenly at the end of a monologue. It is the culmination of a planned activity that leads a customer to a buying decision. At the beginning of the presentation product knowledge benefit statements are given. They are followed later by selling benefit messages. Right from the beginning it is useful to the caller to know whether customer interest is rising or falling.

Obstacles

Question: What kinds of obstacle are met in closing a sale?
Answer: Obstacles to a sale fall into three categories:
              1   Those imposed by the caller.
              2   Those put up by the potential customer to prevent the sale being closed.
              3   Inertia.

Closing is asking for an order whether directly or indirectly. It is the end point of a sales sequence:

Customer qualification → Benefit messages →
                          Objection countering → Close

There are three major types of obstacle that delay or prevent a close:

1   Self-imposed obstacles:
Fear that a direct 'No' will kill the sale or that the presentation is inadequate; doubt that not enough relevant benefit messages have been passed; and worry that the real needs of the potential customer have not yet been identified.

2   Obstacles created by the prospective customer:

(a)   Tendency to delay decision-making. It is much easier to avoid a decision than to make one:
       'Yes. It is certainly attractive. I want to think about it. I will let you know.'

Many people have psychological barriers against making a choice. They delay decision-making until the last possible moment. Even though the customer needs the product or service and is fully aware of the benefits, the decision to buy is put off.

(b)   Fear of the risk involved in decision-making. What happens if the watch, or house, or raincoat is no good? Will friends approve? Is it too much money? Is is fashionable? Post-sale doubt is a much researched concept. It forms the basis of one of the two major theories explaining the effectiveness of advertising.

One school believes that advertising changes attitudes and leads people to buy. The other school believes that the prime role of advertising is to consolidate and reinforce buying decisions that have already been made. For example, a customer buys an expensive car and the next day he or she sees a colour picture of that car displayed in the paper or in a magazine. This creates a warm, comfortable feeling of security.

3   Inertia:
Dislike of change. People grow used to doing things and using things in a particular way. People form habits and feel comfortable with a familiar process and do not want to alter it:
'No. I am sorry. The solvent process has worked satisfactorily for the last ten years. The men are happy with it. I would not like to change.'

Closing

Question: What is the best way to close?
Answer: There are a number of different ways of closing. The most effective of all is to ask for the order and then 'shut up'.

There are a number of different ways of closing and there are no set rules. Experience and judgement guide the caller in selecting the best close to a presentation. Circumstances vary and the experienced seller recognizes which close is most suitable for which customer.

Different forms of closing

The direct shut-up close

The person selling, whether on the telephone or face-to-face, asks for the order directly:

'Will you buy it?'

Then there is silence. Not another word is spoken until the prospective customer answers. In the shut-up close the first person who speaks, loses. The silence seems interminable but this does not matter because the longer the silence continues, the harder it is for the customer to say 'No'. If the customer does not answer immediately then there is tension and, because of this, the caller feels a strong compulsion to add something. Perhaps an extra benefit or a discount will sway the balance – the seller wants to add anything that makes the customer say 'yes'. However, the caller must bite his or her tongue and nothing must be said until the customer speaks.

The shut-up close is very effective. However, because of the strength required to use it, many people prefer to adopt the assumptive close.

The indirect assumptive close

A deliberate assumption is made in the conversation that the customer is going to buy. This avoids the direct close question, which might be refused. If the assumptive close is not taken up or is avoided, the situation is retrievable. It is easier to deal with than a direct 'No'.

'When the motor mower is delivered, it is quite safe for your children to use it. There is an easy instruction booklet.'
'Would you want an invoice in the new financial period?'
'Would you be calling for it?'

In the face-to-face selling situation the indirect assumptive close is not necessarily verbal. It can be conveyed by actions on the seller's part. At an appropriate moment an order pad is picked up and the caller asks:

'How do you spell your name?'
'What is the address?'

The indirect alternative close

The customer is given two product or service alternatives from which to choose. The question as to whether or not the product or service itself is to be selected is sidestepped. So the importance of the decision that the customer has to make is psychologically reduced.

'Would you want the green or the red model?'
'Will you be paying by cash or by cheque?'
'Will you want delivery this week or next?'
'Would you want the machine plumbed in your kitchen or in the boiler house?'

The lock close

This close too, is extremely effective. (It has already been discussed on page 84.) The lock close is most effective in a situation where there is one major obstacle standing in the way of a sale:

Customer   'Is the cutter we saw yesterday safe?'
Representative   'Yes. If 1 demonstrate that the safety factors comply with all the requirements of the Health and Safety Act of 1974, will you buy it?'

The last one close

The person selling has worked hard to achieve a sale but the point where a direct shut-up close seems appropriate has not yet been reached. The intention of the last one close is to create a sense of urgency in the mind of the potential customer. The customer is told that there is only one left:

'Yes, Mr Green. There is one left in stock. The next batch coming in will be at a higher price. If you order it now I can hold it for delivery next month, but will invoice at today's price.'

In the face-to-face situation the close can be equally dramatic. For example, the representative picks up the telephone and he or she dials the stockroom. The important part of the conversation is that which the customer hears. This type of conversation can even be faked – in reality the representative calls a friend or even the speaking clock:

'Hello, stockroom? This is Joe Peters. I am with a client. Is the black trencher model, large size, still in stock? . . . Oh good. Has Mr Grant, who was interested in it, called in with his cheque? . . . No? In that case reserve the model for the next two hours. Don't sell it to anyone else as I am with a client who may wish to buy it.'

The discount method

This close takes full advantage of human weakness. Every customer likes to have a bargain and getting a discount means making a saving. It does not always occur to customers that the discount offered is added into the costing to allow the seller more flexibility:

'Mrs Brown, until you have tried the sun-bed course you just cannot know how effective it is. I want you to try it. As an introductory offer I will give you fifteen per cent discount.'

'Mr Hart, if you order three of the green models and three of the red models I will allow the quantity discounts applicable to bulk quantities.'

'I was at your house yesterday when unfortunately you were called away suddenly. We didn't get round to discussing terms. If you let us install the shower unit we would like to use your house as a demonstration installation since we do not have another installation in your area. For this we can give you a special demonstration discount of twenty per cent.'

However, continuous discount selling is weak selling 'and when planned discounts are exceeded, profitability is eroded. It is best to use the close that is most suitable to the particular type of customer in a particular sales situation. Just because a close works well once does not mean that it will always work in any situation.

The plus and minus method

To reach a buying decision, a customer mentally tots up the positive and negative attributes of the product or service being offered. If the seller fulfils his function successfully, all of the minuses have been neutralized and some have even been converted to plusses. The tools the caller uses are: qualifying questions; benefit statements; objection handling; closing.

At any stage in the presentation, the person selling has only an idea of what the prospective customer is really thinking. Information comes from answers to questions asked and from statements volunteered by the customer. In the face-to-face situation, observation plays a part too. Sometimes even after a long presentation the caller is not sure of what the customer is thinking because feedback information has not been clear. The plus and minus close is an appropriate close for this type of situation perhaps after other closes have already been tried, without success. The plus and minus close can be used on the telephone, although it is even more dramatic in the face-to-face situation. The caller tells the customer to take a clean sheet of paper and to write at the top of the left-hand side of the page, a large 'plus' sign and at the top right-hand side a large 'minus'. The caller directs the conversation along the following lines:

'Mrs Jones, we have talked for a long time about the product and I know you are in the process of arriving at a decision. It is a very difficult decision for you. While there are many positive features – and I hope that I have explained them all to you fully – there are also certain objections.

'Frankly, although I would very much like to have your order, I would rather close this conversation now than have you commit your company to a decision that is not absolutely right. Look. I have a suggestion. In order to clarify the situation, please get a sheet of paper. On the left-hand side write down all the positive features that you can think of. Put down every benefit that your company will have. Then, on the right, write down all the negative features. Put down every disadvantage that you can think of. As you write call out the words, so that I can monitor the situation with you.'

When the customer starts writing on the plus side, the caller gives as much help as possible. Every benefit and every advantage are mentioned and the caller works hard with the customer. When it comes to the minus side, nothing is said. Consequently, the left-hand column list is much shorter:

> *Caller* 'The next step, Mr Jones, is to count the items in the columns.'
>
> *Customer* 'Twenty-three plus features . . . seven minus features.'
>
> *Caller* 'That really makes the decision for you, Mr Jones. It is definitely the correct decision to buy.'

The halo effect close

In this type of close use is made of the halo effect of prestigious customers. The customer is encouraged to copy the buying decisions of a buyer for a much larger concern or to identify his or her decision with that of a person with a famous public image. In this way the fear of making a wrong decision is reduced:

> *Customer* 'Well, I am not convinced that the carpet I saw is the right quality for our main offices.'
>
> *Caller* 'Yes. It is a difficult decision. It is one that Mr Zair, the carpet buyer at British Airways, had to make too. I am proud to say that our carpet is now used for British Airways' entire head office floor area.'
>
> *Customer* 'It certainly looks an attractive car. Yes . . . and it drives smoothly. I cannot make up my mind between this and a Volvo.'
>
> *Representative* 'Yes, it is a difficult decision. Do you remember Peter Sellers the actor? He drove a Saab and Bjorn Borg drives the very model you are looking at. So does George Best. So does Angela Rippon. There is a long list of famous people who drive the Saab Turbo. Even James Bond!'

The emotional pull method

In this close, emotional pressure is applied to make the customer buy:

'Mr Browning, you owe it to your wife and children to have this life assurance policy.'

'Can you be sure that your life will be safe without the Brax safety-belt system?'

The fair play close

When the going has all been uphill and the caller has tried every-thing else, he or she can resort to the fair play close. It is a variation of the emotional pull close, but instead of stressing the advantages of the product or service to the customer, the caller changes the decision to one of a moral nature. Is it fair not to buy, in the light of all the effort made by the caller?

'Mr Browning, can you help me? I have tried, for the last hour while we have been talking together, to describe the ways in which the equipment benefits you and your family. Together, we have also talked about the different ways in which, somehow, you could manage without it.

'I know, from the thousands of customers who have been helped already, that it would give you exceptional help and support. Nevertheless, Mr Browning, we have not yet reached the point where you can firmly make the decision to buy. Tell me, Mr Browning, where have I failed?'

Timing

Question: What is the best time to close?
Answer: There is no set period of time after which the close must be introduced. What is important is that the close is in sequence – after customer needs are satisfied.

In the sales cycle there is no set period of time allocated to each stage of the sequence.

Example

Home extensions costing thousands of pounds are sold to a house-holder in the space of two hours in an evening. Home owners write into the building company after seeing an advertisement for home extensions in a newspaper. A representative then calls, usually without an appointment, and, if the representative is good and well trained, he or she leaves with a signed order and a deposit and the sales cycle is completed. Needs have been identified, product benefits passed, objections met, and the deal has been closed with an order. The time taken for the total sequence is two hours and the close is introduced after about one and three-quarter hours. In that time the representative has totally gained the confidence of the customer and other members of the family present.

Contrast example

In a cold prospecting telephone call an aggressive trade press publisher secures a commitment for a thousand pounds worth of advertising in a period of five to ten minutes. Only a few minutes pass before an effective close is introduced. The organization that places the advertising order has a substantial advertising appropriation and the decision-maker, usually the marketing manager, is a specialist. He or she knows the profile of readers that must be reached. Specific information about price, circulation, readership and competitive publicity is provided as well as relevant details relating to the particular industry requirements.

The seller's function is to achieve early credibility and then to convince the buyer that the benefits are there. If a successful close is not reached in the space of the telephone call, it is unlikely that a subsequent sale will be achieved. The reason for this is that the tele-sales trade press publisher is often a small entrepreneurial company which, of necessity, is highly professional and competent. However, often their resources are small – their premises are perhaps back street. If a telephone call back is made, the customer has had time to think carefully about what has been offered and has had the leisure to compare the image of the trade press publisher with the vital and glossy images of the giants of the industry. The comparison probably inhibits the placing of business with the smaller fry.

The decision-making process undergone by the customer who

buys as a result of a prospecting telephone call is the same in most industries. The telephone selling call must, therefore, always be in the control of the caller, starting with customer qualification and ending with an effective close.

Sometimes, as a deliberate ploy, opening with massive benefits works. It secures interest and the qualification stage can then follow, instead of coming first. The close, however, must always be last and trial closes should be used first.

Not giving up

Question: What should be done if the close is not successful?
Answer: The caller must judge which of two courses of action should be pursued:
1 Treat the refusal as an objection to be countered.
2 Give up and move on to another customer.

Not every sales call is successful and many calls need a lot of skill and great persistence. Selling is not simply order taking. If a customer knows what he or she wants and has the money, all that is needed is to arrange an order. Selling involves exploring customer needs and leading and directing a customer in a controlled way. The culmination is the point where the buying decision is reached.

If a close is unsuccessful, there is a reason and the caller must find that reason. Special skill is necessary. When a close meets with a 'No' there are a number of options:

1 An instinctive reaction is to argue:

'You should buy. It is good for you.'

'Why won't you take it? It is right for your house.'

This approach is counter-productive. On rare occasions it works, depending on the tone and manner of the caller. But usually the customer argues back and the real issue is lost along the way. Often this approach causes anger and irritation in the customer. It is a rule that a customer's value judgement is never directly refuted.

The way round the problem is first to agree and then follow up with a counter-argument:

Customer 'No. It is too big. It does not suit the garden.'
Representative 'I see, Mr Blade. I agree with you that it is large. Do you not think that, in some circumstances, a large visual object complements the proportions of the garden by providing an immediate focus?'

If a customer says something that is factually incorrect, the situation is different. Provided that the caller's tone is not triumphant or offensive, the error may be corrected:

'No, Mr Blade. You are mistaken. It has a three litre engine, not a two litre.'

2   Recognize the refusal as yet another objection to be met:

(a)   The customer's needs are not yet fully known.
(b)   Inadequate benefits have been given.
(c)   Irrelevant benefit messages have been passed.
(d)   The customer's attitude must be changed.
(e)   The customer's interest has been lost.
(f)   The customer has no money.

Applying his or her skill, the caller sets about identifying the real problem, and solving it.

3   Give up. Some calls do end in failure and persistence may prejudice future attempts to sell other products to the same company. Judgement and experience must come into play. If too much time is spent on an unproductive call, it is wasted. It could be employed making other calls that would lead to profitable business.

Summary

Questions	Answers
1 What is a trial close?	A trial close is a technique for testing the progress towards a sale achieved in a presentation.
2 What is a buying signal?	A buying signal is an indication given by the customer – by manner or by what is said – that he or she is interested in what is being offered.
3 What kinds of obstacle are met in closing a sale?	Obstacles to a sale fall into three categories: 1 Those imposed by the caller. 2 Those put up by the potential customer to prevent the sale being closed. 3 Inertia.
4 What is the best way to close?	There are a number of different ways of closing. The most effective of all is to ask for the order and then 'shut up'.
5 What is the best time to close?	There is no set period of time after which the close must be introduced. What is important is that the close is in sequence – after customer needs are satisfied.
6 What should be done if the close is not successful?	The caller must judge which of two courses of action should be pursued: 1 Treat the refusal as an objection to be countered. 2 Give up and move on to another customer.

Chapter 9

How to plan for the repeat sale

There are seven questions below. Each question is worked through and answered in the chapter. Answer the questions before reading this chapter. There is a summary at the end of the chapter giving the questions and answers together.

Questions	Answers
1 What is the value of a follow-up call?	
2 What happens if the follow-up call is traditionally a visit, not a telephone call?	
3 What format should the follow-up call take?	
4 What benefits apart from repeat business are derived from a satisfied customer?	
5 What is the way to make customers satisfied?	
6 How far should the manu-facturer be concerned that the company's products are being used correctly?	
7 What is the best way to handle complaints?	

Chapter 9　How to plan for the repeat sale

Follow-up – Changing the natural order – The way to do it – The satisfied customer – How customers are satisfied – Correct product usage – Handling complaints – Summary.

Follow-up

Question:　What is the value of a follow-up call?
Answer:　For the customer a follow-up call is an opportunity:
　　　　1　To advise on any immediate problems with the delivery.
　　　　2　To pass any repeat order instructions.
　　　　For the supplier the follow-up call maintains good communication between supplier and customer.

In simple terms the business cycle is:

$$\text{Payment} \xrightarrow{} \text{Customer order} \xrightarrow{} \text{Manufacture}$$
$$\xleftarrow{} \text{Delivery} \xleftarrow{}$$

The four constituent acitivities provide the bare bones of the cycle. There are other subordinate activities which make up each constituent. For example, the customer order is often the end point of a co-ordinated sequence of activities, involving personnel, cost and management skill. Similarly, in many industry business cycles, the manufacture stage is represented by the holding of stock.

Business profits stem from the smooth and efficient repetition of the cycle. Efficiency requires good communication between supplier and customer. A follow-up call after each delivery is good communication. Where the delivery is concerned, each side has different needs.

Customer needs: Delivery of order precisely as specified.
Delivery on time.
Uniform high quality level of delivered goods or service.
Possible requirements additional to those ordered.

Supplier needs: Payment for goods.
Confirmation that customer is satisfied and pleased with goods or service.
Repeat order.

If a follow-up call is not made by a supplier, the business cycle may still be repeated. Provided, that is, that the delivery is to a standard acceptable to the customer.

Follow-up rule
A supplier should always telephone after a delivery to ensure that all is as it should be.

Changing the natural order

Question: What happens if the follow-up call is traditionally a visit, not a telephone call?

Answer: It is difficult to change long-standing traditions. Changes in procedure must be introduced when business is started with new clients.

In many industries it is established practice for a representative to call on a customer after a delivery. He or she discusses any problems and takes further orders.

Example Feedstuffs and seeds delivered by a producer to farmers. The farmer knows what quantities are necessary to feed his livestock and could easily telephone his order. Alternatively, a written order in the post could be sent to the supplier. In practice, neither of these things happen because, by tradition, a representative calls at the farm. If he or she does not call, there is no repeat order because the competition is always calling to woo business from the farmer.

Logically, a change from tradition to taking the repeat business by phone would be productive and progressive. The representative would have time released for further selling and the farmer would save the time spent in discussion. The time involved in making a call at the farm is rarely less than half an hour and this takes no account of the representative's journey.

Realistically, it is unlikely that farmers will suddenly change their habit of years. The representative who announces to the farmer, after years of calling, that he proposes telephoning instead, cannot be assured of a very good reception. Instead, the representative must plan to bring about the change. The time to introduce the new arrangements is when a new account is opened. The benefits to the farmer are sold in the same way that the product benefits are sold:

'Thank you, Mr Giles. The yield from our wheat cake is eight per cent greater – according to our customers who used it last year. It is a good decision to try it with your animals. Mr Giles, I have a suggestion to make. Normally, I would call on you in ten days time when you would have about five days feed supply left. If I were to telephone you instead on that day, at lunch time, it would save interrupting your milking and harvesting schedules. I know how busy you are at this time of the year. When we speak on the phone you could tell me what you need. Do you think that this proposal would help you by saving your time?'

The way to do it

Question: What format should the follow-up call take?
Answer: There are six distinct stages to the follow-up call:
1   Introduction.
2   Remind customer of previous order.
3   Pass fresh benefit messages.
4   Get feedback.
5   Counter objections.
6   Close for repeat order.

As with all business telephone calls, the follow-up call is planned in advance. The format is as follows:

Introduction

The customer must be addressed by name. As a general rule, avoid superfluous chat. There are exceptions, for example, personal events or achievements which the customer is proud of may be mentioned:

'Hello, Mr Jones. This is Tom Redfern of Utol Copiers Ltd. You gave us your order last month for the 794 series equipment. By the way, I hear you have received another Queen's Award, this month. . . .'

The personal information is not necessarily recalled from memory but is part of the information carefully recorded by the caller immediately after each conversation. Keeping customer index cards is the best way of doing this. The following information should appear:

Client name, address, telephone number and extension number
Name of personal contact
Status of contact
Order placed – details – date – value
Objections raised
Client problems
Client interests

Remind customer of previous order placed and subjects discussed

There are always key discussion areas which lead up to an order being placed. Memory of these is stimulated by using a few key words:

'Hello Mr Jones. This is Tom Redfern of Utol Copiers Ltd. You gave us your order for the 794 series equipment. If you remember, we discussed the problem of the export department documentation and also the difficulties with colour reproduction. . . .'

154

The customer is taken back, effectively, to his or her decision-making process when placing the previous order.

Pass fresh benefit messages

Benefit statements are used to consolidate the earlier sale – even though it is delivered and paid for. The benefits are also of some use in pre-empting any objections that are about to be levelled at the caller. It is unlikely that every single benefit was used at the previous meeting:

'. . . and the installation was completed for you last week, Mr Jones. Have you had a chance to inspect the new ink-feed section? It is part of your new equipment and gives absolutely constant quality reproduction – with runs of thousands.'

Obtain feedback of success with order

If there is a problem, genuine or imagined, the customer usually states the complaint as soon as the caller's name is given. When this happens, the complaint must not be brushed aside. It is an objection and it is important to the customer.

Even without major objections there are a number of situations that stand in the way of repeat business:

1   Goods not sold.
2   Interest of customer's own clients has waned.
3   Merchandise not displayed properly.
4   Merchandise damaged or defective.
5   Other merchandise absorbing more sales attention from staff.
6   Insufficient point of sale material.
7   Inadequate staff training.
8   Customer's other merchandise more competitive.

Counter any complaints

The solution to most objections raised against a supplier's delivery lies in making concessions. It is easy for a caller to offer a discount.

155

It is a quick solution and it takes a caller past an unpleasant part of a follow-up call. But a discount also erodes profitability and it must not, therefore, be given easily. Sometimes complaints are fabricated, although this does not often happen.

Every complaint must be considered on its own merits. If an order is to be the end point of the follow-up call, all complaints must be resolved. When the issues are small, commercial practice dictates that suppliers give way, even when the complaint is unjustified. To gain further business it is worth making the sacrifice. The objective is for the customer to be satisfied.

It should be the general rule to anticipate customer complaints and to compute, in advance, discretionary discounts applicable to product deliveries. Most suppliers do not normally expect complaints against deliveries but they do, however, occur.

The close for a repeat order

The customer is satisfied with the delivered order and any problems have been resolved. It is therefore now time to ask for repeat business. For repeat business use the direct shut-up close. It is the most appropriate close to use now that doubts and uncertainties shrouding the initial order have been overcome. The use of any other form of closing in this situation is a sign of weakness:

'Will you buy some more?'

'May I send in the same quantity next month?'

The satisfied customer

Question: What benefits apart from repeat business are derived from a satisfied customer?

Answer: The satisfied customer contributes to the growth and expansion of business in two important ways:
1 Facilitates an efficient operation.
2 Provides an effective marketing referent.

The benefits of having satisfied customers are:

1 Prompt payment of bills.
2 Recommendation to other sources of business.
3 An increasing volume of business as the relationship continues.
4 Referent for marketing purposes with new customers:

'. . . and we have supplied Chalk Brothers Ltd for many years. They find the ZZ223 design a very profitable line. Will you stock it?'

With a satisfied customer there is a good relationship between the supplier and the customer and this counts when problems occur. Problems do occur with good and with bad customers but when the relationship is solid and when communication lines are open there is little or no rancour or animosity. Differences are considered, discussed and resolved.

How customers are satisfied

Question: What is the way to make customers satisfied?
Answer: The route to customer satisfaction lies in sound communication and reliable and efficient service.

Satisfied customers do not just happen. They have to be created. The supplier must work hard on a number of fronts:

1 Efficient administration.
   (a) Acknowledgement of orders received.
       Basic business courtesy must not be overlooked with long-standing customers. It is efficient to acknowledge orders and the customer has confirmation that his or her requirements are being processed.
   (b) Correct processing of orders.
       The processing is an internal activity. Customer instructions, amendments or special requirements should not be allowed to go astray. Good relationships are strained when mistakes occur.
   (c) Return of telephone call messages.
       If the customer calls and does not make contact with the wanted person but leaves a message, then the message must reach that person. An appropriate procedure, under-

stood and practised by everyone in the company, will meet this requirement.

When the person called is very busy, the temptation to delay calling back should be resisted. If delay cannot be avoided the customer's call message must not be submerged and lost beneath more recent overwhelming day-to-day demands.

2   Advising the customer of new products and developments.
A satisfied customer is not an entity on its own but part of a two-way relationship. Both sides benefit from successful mutual activities. Good customers must continually be kept up to date about new products and developments. More importantly, the comments and reactions of a client company are valuable customer feedback. With new products much research is necessary to get the product right and successful marketing depends on continual market feedback reports. It should therefore be made a rule to keep established customers abreast of new products and, wherever possible, to involve them in product development.

3   Referral of retail customers' enquiries.
There are four principal ways in which manufacturers and suppliers promote their products and services:
(a)   Individual company advertising through the media, either nationally or regionally, naming the retail outlets.
(b)   Advertising of the concept by industry or trade association.
         Examples   Milk Marketing Board – 'Drinka pinta milk'
                              Egg Marketing Board – 'Go to work on an egg'
         Different producers combine with the industry to advertise the basic concept and it is left to the individual suppliers to win business as a result of motivated customers.
(c)   Manufacturers concentrate on product quality and benefit and individual outlets are left to generate business through their own personal selling efforts.
(d)   'Missionary selling': this method originated in the USA and, though used in the UK, is not widespread as yet. The manufacturer employs a team of representatives to sell the company products. Orders are not taken directly but are referred to dealers and distributors.

In all cases there is the possibility that the end user makes contact with the actual manufacturer. The situation arises because:
1   The customer seeks a place to buy.
2   The customer hopes to get the product cheaper from the manufacturer.
If the manufacturer sells direct there is a larger profit made. There is the manufacturer's own margin plus that of whichever distribution channel element has been cut out. It is, however, bad commercial practice to take business away from a manufacturer's outlets.

Rule: Always refer customer enquiries to distribution outlets.

4   Regular contact apart from order taking.
With new customers there is a rule – Get to the business straightaway and cut out social chat. The rule changes, however, when relationships develop. Customers lose their 'customer' status and become more like friends:

'Hello, John. Did you have a good weekend?'

This is a warm and friendly opening to a telephone conversation and is far more preferable to the straightforward:

'Good morning, Mr Winters. My name is. . . .'

The caller's offer in the first example is more likely to attract interest and attention. Intimate friendships with everyone you speak to on the phone is neither feasible nor desirable. But it is possible to develop business friendships which do not transcend the limits of the business relationship. The business friendship is established by a friendly manner and by showing a personal interest in the welfare of the person at the other end of the telephone.

Rule: With discretion, cultivate friendships with regular contacts.

Correct product usage

Question: How far should the manufacturer be concerned that the company's products are being used correctly?

Answer: Correct product usage is very important. Incorrect usage leads to irritation and complaint and inhibits repeat business.

Many products, especially equipment, require skill to use. Personnel in the supplying company develop good usage skills. They become adept at handling the product and take the skill and knowledge they have acquired for granted. For this reason, difficulties experienced by first-time users are frequently overlooked.

New customers probably see a demonstration of the product or equipment in a showroom. Delivery of the ordered equipment is accompanied by printed instructions. However, many non-technical people have difficulty in interpreting written instructions and are reluctant to admit the fact. Difficulty with the new equipment causes frustration and irritation, rapidly followed by anger.

Rule: With all mechanical or electrical products or self-operated services, follow up delivery with a phone call.

Example

Caller 'Hello, Mrs Keeting. Roger Smith of Hotbar Heating Ltd. We have delivered and installed your washing machine. Our engineer demonstrated the procedures to your son. He appeared to be satisfied that he could operate it. I imagine, however, that it is not your son who will be doing all the washing. Are you happy with the loading and programming procedures?'

Customer 'Yes.'

Caller 'You are familiar with the different operations for different materials?'

Customer 'Yes.'

Caller 'Good. The model really is the best. It will give marvellous service. I just wanted to be sure that you are using it correctly. Goodbye.'

Customers using a product for the first time do not necessarily know whether maximum benefit is being obtained. Incorrect operation may allow the machine to work without achieving the benefits for which the product or equipment was specifically purchased.

Example: The American retailer's follow-up system

Scenario   Small American town.
Actors   Customers, television retailer.

A customer shows interest in a colour television set. The retailer satisfies himself that cash or deferred payment terms are within the means of the customer. The retailer then offers a free installation period in the customer's home. The retailer stresses that all the family, especially the children, must be satisfied with the reception.

An engineer installs the set and leaves it in good working order. After a week, the retailer telephones the customer. The customer expects to be asked to make a decision on whether the set is to be bought or is to be returned. Instead, the retailer asks only about the quality of reception. Was the customer quite sure that the tuning adjustments gave the best possible picture?

Two weeks later, the retailer phones the customer for a buying decision. By this time the television has become a fixture in the house. The neighbourhood children have seen it and discussed it. The children are proud to have something that others want to see. The decision for the home owner is now much more weighted. It is no longer just a question of spending a sum of money, or not. The neighbours would know that the set had been sent back. The children would be deprived of a benefit to which they had grown accustomed.

For three years running the retailer using this ploy won the manufacturer's prize for selling the most television sets in the state.

Handling complaints

Question: What is the best way to handle complaints?
Answer: No matter what the complaint, listen and be diplomatic. Find out and give information and advice and, where expedient, give a discretionary discount.

Complaints arise for a large number of reasons. They fall, however, into a small number of categories:

1 Late delivery
2 Damage
3 Incorrect delivery
4 Accounting errors
5 Cost
6 Delay
7 Personnel
8 Inadequate communication

Rule 1   Listen to what is said.

Until all the information is available, it is wrong to make a judgement. Frequently a holding operation is necessary:

> 'Mr Sykes, I hear what you are saying. I am very sorry for the trouble that you are being given. I cannot really comment until I find out what has taken place at this end. Please bear with me. I will make enquiries immediately and I will call you back as soon as I am in possession of all the facts.'

The fault may lie with:

Suppliers
Contract packers
Warehouse
Carriers
Company personnel

Malpractice occurs too. It can happen anywhere along the line from supplier to consumer but, whatever the reason, the supplier should still listen. Until all the facts are known, nothing should be done precipitantly.

Rule 2:   Be diplomatic.

Overcoming a complaint at the cost of future business is bad business. Customers do not like to be given evidence that they are in the wrong. If the situation occurs be diplomatic.

Customers with a complaint are frequently angry and they will remonstrate with anyone in the supplier company to whom they speak. Customer calls are usually put through to the representative because it is he or she who provides the link between customer and supplier. Usually the fault does not lie with the representative and he or she may know nothing of the mishap, until accused by the angry customer.

If a representative is under pressure, a bluff will get the angry customer off the telephone but it is short-term relief. Bluffs usually rebound. When the correct answer to explain the cause of the customer's complaint is not known, the customer should be told so, diplomatically and a promise of immediate action should follow.

Rule 3:   Find out and give information and advice.

Customers with complaints frequently undergo instant personality changes. They display injured dignity, hurt feelings, distantness and many other expressions of the injury they feel. Allowances and discounts work wonders. They are a panacea.

Rule 4:   Give way on small matters. Be firm on important issues.

Summary

Questions	Answers
1 What is the value of a follow-up call?	For the customer a follow-up call is an opportunity: 1 To advise on any immediate problems with the delivery. 2 To pass any repeat order instructions. For the supplier the follow-up call maintains good communication between supplier and customer.
2 What happens if the follow-up call is traditionally a visit, not a telephone call?	It is difficult to change long-standing traditions. Changes in procedure must be introduced when business is started with new clients.
3 What format should the follow-up call take?	There are six distinct stages to the follow-up call: 1 Introduction. 2 Remind customer of previous order. 3 Pass fresh benefit messages. 4 Get feedback. 5 Counter objections. 6 Close for repeat order.
4 What benefits apart from repeat business are derived from a satisfied customer?	The satisfied customer contributes to the growth and expansion of business in two important ways: 1 Facilitates an efficient operation. 2 Provides an effective marketing referent.
5 What is the way to make customers satisfied?	The route to customer satisfaction lies in sound communication and reliable and efficient service.
6 How far should the manufacturer be concerned that	Correct product usage is very important. Incorrect usage

Questions	*Answers*
the company's products are being used correctly?	leads to irritation and complaint and inhibits repeat business.
7 What is the best way to handle complaints?	No matter what the complaint, listen and be diplomatic. Find out and give information and advice and, where expedient, give a discretionary discount.

Chapter 10

How to answer the telephone

Answer the questions below. After reading this chapter answer the questions again. Check your answers with the summary at the end of the chapter.

Questions	Answers
1 What is the telephone caller's Achilles' heel?	
2 How is the unexpected planned?	
3 Why are orders lost on the telephone?	
4 What are the rules for answering the phone?	
5 What has telephoning got to do with public relations?	

Chapter 10   How to answer the telephone

Caught unawares – How did the order slip away? – To say, or not to say? – PR element – Summary

Caught unawares

Question: What is the telephone caller's Achilles' heel?
Answer: The incoming call that catches the caller unprepared.

Telephone prospecting uses a script. A follow-up call is planned in advance. Getting repeat business is also subject to a plan. The skill of telephoning involves extensive and careful planning at all stages. Incoming calls, however, are not in the control of the caller.

Question: How is the unexpected planned?
Answer: Being aware that it is possible to be caught on the hop is the first step. Preparation is then made to meet the full range of incoming calls that are received.

Incoming calls are not neatly wrapped and labelled. The purpose of the call is only revealed when the person answering the incoming calls enters into conversation with the caller. Incoming calls fall into a number of different categories:
1   Customers seeking product information.
    If the information is known, the call is straightforward. A problem arises when information which should be known is not. The first task of a manager or representative is to establish personal credibility with the customer. If the person answering the phone is found not to have sound product knowledge, the customer's confidence in that person and in the company may be lowered. The company training may appear to be inade-

quate, and the customer may think that perhaps this is sympto-
matic of other inadequacies.

A straightforward reaction, if the answer is not known, is to
promise to supply the information shortly. If that approach is
not expedient, it does not help to tell lies. It is helpful to be
creative and to try to help the customer as much as possible.

Rule: Every answer must be positive.

Example

'Yes, Mr Major. The functions of the small knobs in the rear
panel? Do you know your question is quite a coincidence. I
was running through the performance cycle in my mind over
lunch. I became aware that I did not know the function of
those very knobs. I have a break in my meetings this afternoon and it was my intention to solve that information gap
then. I will come back to you later in the day, with the
information, if I may?'

2 Customers asking for delivery details.
A customer cannot expect everyone in the supplying company
to know about delivery details. If the information is not known,
the caller should be told that he or she will have to wait a
moment while the information is looked up. Wherever possible, transfer the call to another person who is able to help
immediately.

3 Complaints.
The ways of dealing with complaints have been explained in
Chapter 9. The rules are:

Rule 1: Listen to what is said.
Rule 2: Be diplomatic.
Rule 3: Find out and give information and advice.
Rule 4: Give way on small matters. Be firm on important
issues.

4 Accounting queries.
The situation is the same as with customers asking for delivery
details and the procedure is the same.

5 Decision-seeking call.
There are no half measures. The enquirer asks for a positive
decision or statement. In this situation there is no room for a
creative answer. There are only two options:

(a) Give the decision.
(b) Explain that a delay is inevitable, pending a decision being obtained.

6 Time-consuming calls when busy.

It happens to everyone – a pleasant, well-meaning person is on the other end of the line but time is pressing. What is to be done without causing offence? There is no substitute for the truth – tell the caller of the pressing work you were in the middle of when the call came through. Soften the abrupt closing of the conversation with a promise to call back soon.

How did the order slip away?

Question: Why are orders lost on the telephone?
Answer: Orders are lost on the telephone for two major reasons:
   1 Lack of preparation for all types of incoming call.
   2 Inefficient response to customer questions. Replies must sell, in addition to providing product knowledge.

Some of the customers who wish to place an order say so at the beginning of the conversation. With this type of customer there is no problem. Details are taken and the order is processed.

Others ask questions first. They seek information and, as a result of the information given, the customer may reach a decision to place an order. The objectives of the specific questions that customers ask fall into three categories:

1 Satisfaction of an administrative query.

'We bought suction pads from you last year. What sizes are you stocking now?'

The customer needs information on some aspect of past or pending business. What is the reason for the customer's enquiry? Is it a buying signal? What are the customer's current needs? The answer to the question asked by the caller must be linked with qualification of possible needs:

Customer 'We bought suction pads from you last year. What sizes are you stocking now?'

Representative   'As last year we are stocking the full range of sizes, from three centimetres to thirty centimetres. May I ask for what use the pads are needed?'

Rule: Answers to customers' administrative enquiries must be linked to questions qualifying needs.

2   Arriving at a decision to buy.
When a caller needs a product or service, there are two kinds of query that arise:
(a)   The caller does not know whether the company product will fit the bill.
(b)   He or she does not yet know whether the company has the capacity or personnel to supply their needs.
Full product or service information should be given in answer to these queries. In many companies such information is too complex and extensive to be carried in the head.

Rule: Price lists, product information lists and specification details should always be kept adjacent to the telephone.

It is important to have factual information always to hand. When a buying wish is indicated, prompt action is imperative. Delays involving a reply by post or a subsequent telephone call must be avoided. Delay gives the competition an opportunity to intrude. There is a chance that fresh objections will inhibit the decision to buy and the order slips away.

3   Arriving at a decision not to buy.
The customer asks a question and the information is supplied. For the customer it destroys the buying interest. He or she believes their decision is realistic. However, there may be other product benefits that would satisfy the caller's needs. The wrong questions may have been asked by the customer.

Rule 1:   Before supplying information, identify the context in which it is required.

Example
'Yes, sir. I am certainly able to give you the answers. Before I do, may I ask what exactly you intend to use the machine for? The performance figures relate to different usage situations.'

A customer question is a potential buying question. So answers to specific questions should not simply be product knowledge answers. There should be powerful selling benefit statements too.

Answer 1

   Customer 'I have heard that you offer a Universal set of tools. What is it like?'

   Representative 'Oh yes, sir. The Universal Multipack set of tools contains fourteen spanners and costs twenty-three pounds fifty.'

   Customer 'I see. I don't want it thanks.'

Answer 2

   Customer 'I have heard that you offer a Universal set of tools. What is it like?'

   Representative 'Oh yes, sir. The Universal Multipack set of tools has fourteen spanners. It has been designed so that every single size of nut and bolt on the market can be dealt with using this one set. Furthermore, all of the spanners have been magnetized so that they can retrieve nuts that fall into difficult positions. The Multipack carries a five year guarantee and costs only twenty-three pounds fifty. If you built up a set yourself to carry out the same function, it would cost at least thirty-five pounds.'

   Customer It sounds interesting. I must certainly try out this line.'

Rule 2: When supplying information against a customer's question, sell.

To say, or not to say?

Question: What are the rules for answering the phone?

Answer: State the subscriber's number, company name or your name, as appropriate to the type of telephone or extension.

When the telephone rings, the majority of people pick up the receiver and say 'Hello'. This is friendly but does not give enough information. There are different types of telephone call that need answering:

(a) An outside line.

   Rule: Respond by giving the subscriber's number.

(b) The subscriber is a company and no other company uses that line.

   Rule: State the company name.

   Some large companies, employing switchboard operators, have a standard greeting:

   '732 9876. The Browning Tool Company. Good morning.'

(c) An internal line – When the telephone is connected to a switchboard obviously there is no point in giving the company's name or the subscriber number. The switchboard operator stands between the outside caller and whoever answers the telephone.

   Rule: The person who answers states his or her name.

   Adding a first name to a surname is optional.

Frequently there are many extensions in a tele-sales office. There is much activity as, throughout the day, representatives try to sell. Incoming calls are invariably from customers or potential customers. When a call is answered the representative must work hard to sell. The customer must not only be allowed to have the information that he or she requested. A commitment must be obtained from the caller to agree to one of the following options:

(a) To buy.
(b) To sample.
(c) To send an official order.
(d) To send a telex or cable confirmation.
(e) To send a cheque.
(f) To accept literature.
(g) To call at the company office or showroom.
(h) To telephone back.
(i) To write in with full details of enquiry.
(j) To agree to an appointment for a representative to call.

Rule: Never give neutral information to an incoming caller. Obtain the caller's positive commitment towards a sale.

General dos and don'ts

Dos

Do speak clearly.
Do be courteous.
Do be business-like.
Do always have a notepad and pencil handy.
Do memorize the subscriber number.
Do be positive.
Do memorize the caller's name and use it in the conversation.

Don'ts

Don't mumble.
Don't leave the caller hanging on for long periods.
Don't deviate from the planned telephone procedure.
Don't eat or drink while talking.
Don't shout.

The PR element

Question: What has telephoning got to do with public relations?
Answer: Every spoken contact with the outside world is a potential public relations statement. The telephone user must take care that a sloppy telephone technique does not create a bad PR image.

The function of advertising is creative. It attempts to change attitudes, to manipulate buying decisions and to confirm buying decisions already made. Public relations has a different function.

The PR activities of a company are bringing awareness of that company and all that it does to the attention of the public. In smaller companies, attention to PR activities is spasmodic or non-existent. As companies grow in size, PR requirements increase and an officer is appointed to a post which is devoted entirely to promoting the PR image. Related functions of this post are producing house magazines and producing product and packaging publicity. The PR officer generates interest by releasing infor-

173

mation on company news and developments through the media. They are directed either to the general public, or to a specific trade segment, or to both.

Advertisements in the media are paid for by the sponsor but PR releases are accepted free. There is also no charge for the useful PR statements made in telephone calls to customers. Such statements are part of the PR function and very many are made every day and all day. Frequently little attention is paid by companies to the image created by employee habits.

The PR image on the telephone is created in two ways:

1   By telephone manner.

A person with a clear, business-like, friendly telephone manner is remembered. So is the person who swears, speaks hesitantly or is ignorant of his or her company policy and activities.

Customers identify employees with their company. It is not Tom Jones who swears, speaks indistinctly and is ill informed. It is his company that is inefficient and unpleasant.

Rule: Remember that every telephone call reflects not only the caller's image but that of his or her company as well. At all times be positive and business-like.

2   By what is said.

PR announcements promoting the company image can be introduced deliberately into conversations. The lead-in for a PR announcement is:

'By the way, did you know . . . ?'

A factual statement which is relevant to the customer's or incoming caller's interests and needs makes a useful contribution to marketing and selling.

Examples

'We are now supplying the Central Electricity Board.'

'Last year sixty per cent of our business was to export markets.'

'Our products are advertised on television.'

'The military are conducting a feasibility study on this particular weapon.'

'Our division won the annual company award for overall fastest turn round.'

174

'Tom Brown in the sales division was capped for England at rugby.'

PR throw-away lines have most value with new customers or potential customers. They increase credibility.

Rule: Prepare a selection of informative and interesting items of company news. Introduce appropriate items with new and potential customers.

Summary

Questions	Answers
1 What is the telephone caller's Achilles' heel?	The incoming call that catches the caller unprepared.
2 How is the unexpected planned?	Being aware that it is possible to be caught on the hop is the first step. Preparation is then made to meet the full range of incoming calls that are received.
3 Why are orders lost on the telephone?	Orders are lost on the telephone for two major reasons: 1 Lack of preparation for all types of incoming call. 2 Inefficient response to customer questions. Replies must sell in addition to providing product knowledge.
4 What are the rules for answering the phone?	State the subscriber's number, company name or your name, as appropriate to the type of telephone or extension.
5 What has telephoning got to do with public relations?	Every spoken contact with the outside world is a potential public relations statement. The telephone user must take care that a sloppy telephone technique does not create a bad PR image.

How to write the follow-up letter

As with the other chapters, read and answer the following questions before reading this chapter. There is a summary of questions and answers at the end of the chapter.

Questions   **Answers**

1   What is the function of the follow-up letter?
2   What is the correct way to confirm an order taken on the telephone?
3   What is the best formula for writing the prospecting letter?
4   What factors govern the number of letters that should be written?

Chapter 11   How to write the follow-up letter

Function of the follow-up letter – Order confirmation – About prospecting letters – How to write the prospecting letter – How many letters? – Summary

Function of the follow-up letter

Question: What is the function of the follow-up letter?
Answer: The follow-up letter has two functions:
         1   To confirm in writing an agreement reached on the telephone.
         2   To reopen a discussion or tentative agreement which has taken place on the phone by setting out the salient features.

Appointments

When an appointment is arranged on the telephone, it is good business practice to follow it up with a letter. Memory is unreliable. A written statement that the appointment has been made confirms the arrangement both for the customer and for the caller.

Example

Dear Mr Browning

Following our telephone conversation today, I write to confirm our meeting on Tuesday next, 24th April. I will call on you at your Piccadilly offices at 10.00 a.m. I look forward to seeing you.

Yours sincerely

The letter is a personal one because an intimacy was established through the conversation. 'Dear Mr . . .' letters always finish with 'Yours sincerely'. In the letter it is unnecessary to add benefit messages. Nor should the letter be padded out in any way. The content is factual – there is going to be an opportunity at the meeting to sell or to discuss other matters. It is acceptable to add good wishes and perhaps an expression of pleasure in anticipation of the event.

Resuscitating a discussion

Discussions on the phone may, for a variety of reasons, end without agreement being reached. The reasons may be:

Insufficient information
Inadequate resources
Lack of time
Priority of other work
Inadequate personnel
Wrong environmental conditions

The list could be longer. The caller wants to create an opportunity to continue the discussion. A length of time has been allowed to elapse and conditions may have altered. The follow-up letter sets out the salient points of the discussion and it proposes or suggests fresh ways of continuing the discussion.

Example

Dear Mr Browning

I am writing with regard to our earlier discussion on the telephone regarding the tunnel extension. A meeting was arranged between us three months ago but was cancelled owing to your pressure of work. I now have fresh structural calculations. Could we meet at a convenient time soon to see if progress can be made?

Yours sincerely

Order confirmation

Question: What is the correct way to confirm an order taken on the telephone?

Answer: The order confirmation should set out on headed paper all the relevant details of the order instruction. The major details are price, quantity, specification, delivery period, packaging, operating instructions, delivery instructions, payment terms, guarantee and warranty conditions.

Every order taken on the telephone must be confirmed in writing. Companies taking a lot of business in this way find a standard printed order confirmation helpful. When this is not the case, the follow-up letter sets out the precise details that have been agreed. When there is no conflicting company policy or precedent, an order confirmation should be written on a separate sheet of headed paper which is then attached to an accompanying letter. Even when the order has been placed during an informal friendly conversation, the order confirmation needs to be formal and business-like.

Example1

Dear Mr Goldring

It was delightful to talk to you again after ten years. I am glad that your family are all well. Before anything else, let me thank you for the order you placed. I enclose with this letter our confirmation of the details.

Now, to return to personal matters. . . .

Confirmation of telephone order

Client:	Mr Goldring. Pertwen Products Ltd
Date:	27th April 1983
Product:	China clay earthenware mugs. Packed 6 mugs per carton.
Quantity:	100 cartons of 6 mugs. Total 600 mugs.
Price:	60 pence per mug. Packing included. Delivered to warehouse.
Delivery:	10th May 1983.

Payment terms   Monthly account.

per pro FIDDEN CHINA PRODUCTS LTD

. . . .
Director

About prospecting letters

There are a number of important differences between prospecting for business by letter and prospecting by phone:

1   The prospecting letter is a permanent record. The company that is interested in what is offered will file the letter and keep it available for reference at a later date. With the phone call, the memory of the call fades and often memory distorts.
2   Every part of the prospecting letter counts. One word misspelt or grammatically incorrect spoils the whole effect. Each word used makes its contribution to the whole and no word should be wasted.
3   There are legal obligations with letters. The written word has greater authority than the spoken word and an offer embodied in a sales letter carries legal obligations which are binding on both parties. If the same offer is made verbally, any contract that is established is more difficult to substantiate. However, a contract made over the phone is none the less binding, if the company is to keep its good name.
4   There are literary demands on the author of a prospecting letter but in other respects it is an easier approach to make to a potential customer. There is no 'moment of truth' when the customer at the other end of the line answers. Inexperienced persons, when making their first telephone prospecting calls, often sweat and their throat becomes dry. Frequently they experience a very real feeling of sickness in the stomach. This is a hurdle that salespeople must overcome when telephone prospecting. The problems disappear, for most people, as soon as the first objective is achieved.

How to write the prospecting letter

Question: What is the best formula for writing a prospecting letter?

Answer: The formula lies in a set of key *rules* which apply to all industries and professions.

In order to create rules, pertinent questions are asked and, from the answers, the rules are formulated.

Question: What are the objectives of the prospecting letter?

Answer: Either a sale is being sought or an appointment to visit and present an offer. The objective governs the format of the letter.

Key rule 1
Identify the objectives of the prospecting letter.

Question: To whom should the letter be addressed?

Answer: All prospecting letters are personal letters. The impact necessary to motivate a customer to buy is rarely achieved by writing to a Mr Managing Director or to a Mr Purchasing Officer. This means that research is necessary to establish the correct details. If the information is not available from a directory or other publication, a telephone call to the company should be made to ask for the information.

Example

'Hello, is that the Hydraulic Machinery Company Limited? I am writing to the person responsible for purchasing replacement parts for hydraulic equipment. Would you kindly tell me his name and initials and exact title in the company?'

To avoid being put through to the buyer, something else should be added. Otherwise the caller may be precipitated into a call for which he or she is not prepared:

'I do not want to speak to him at the present time, so please do not put me through.'

The correct method of address, when the name is obtained is:
Mr William D. Blow, MBIM
Purchasing Officer
Hydraulic Machinery Company Limited
The High Place
Slough
Bucks BF1 22Y

Dear Mr Blow

. . . .

Yours sincerely

Everyone likes to see their name and title or qualifications recognized, if they do not use them themselves at all times. For this reason, qualifications and full job title should be used.

Key rule 2
Address the customer personally by name, initials, qualifications and title.

Question: Who is it that is making contact?
Answer: The customer must be introduced to the writer of the letter.

Sometimes a letter heading gives sufficient information. However when the title is general in nature, additional information is relevant and necessary. The initial introduction should also include a reference to the specific area of activity in which the customer is assessed to be interested.

Example

Puresound Radio Company Ltd
14 Brown Street
Redhill
6th June 1983

Mr Ronnie Packard
General Manager
Bedroom Hotel
High Street
Redhill

Dear Mr Packard

I am writing to introduce our company as your local distributor for the Bleep Bleep paging system. This week Bleep Bleep Ltd have launched their revolutionary, button-hole size, paging unit. It combines the functions of both transmitter and receiver.

The new miniaturized system has pioneered new frontiers of technology. The Bleep Bleep system now permits multi-way transmission between users and central control. There is no recourse to telephone or bulky transmitters. The Bleep Bleep unit measures 5mm by 10mm and may be worn in the button-hole of a jacket or pinned to a dress.

To demonstrate its wide application and reliable high performance, Bleep Bleep offer a 24 hour trial installation. It is absolutely free of charge with no obligation whatsoever.

If you decide, at the end of the trial period, that the Bleep Bleep system cannot offer time-reducing savings in manpower activities – with increased lower cost communication efficiency – Bleep Bleep Ltd will remove their equipment. No charge will be made at all.

I will telephone you in a few days time to discuss the best uses that might be made of the Bleep Bleep paging system. During the free installation period I will of course be available to answer any queries that arise.

Yours sincerely

Ian Pushar
Sales Executive

Key rule 3
Introduce writer and company.

Question: How is the interest of the customer gained and held?
Answer: Customer interest is essential. It is a prerequisite of the writer achieving his or her objective. The customer must be told why the letter has been written.

In the sample letter above, Bleep Bleep state why they are writing – they have launched an exciting new product.

Key rule 4
Give a reason for writing.

Question: What kinds of benefit should be offered?
Answer: When a prospecting letter is sent, an assumption is made regarding the needs of the person or company to whom the letter is sent. It is those needs that will be satisfied by the offer made. If the needs prove to be real, success may follow.

In respect of Bedroom Hotel, in the sample letter, two assumptions are made:
1   That the hotel management has an on-going requirement to communicate with its staff in different parts of the hotel.
2   That some members of staff frequently require to speak to other members.
The message that is incorporated into the prospecting letter relates to the assumed needs and offers a means of giving satisfaction.

Key rule 5
Offer benefits that satisfy the prospective customer's assessed needs.

Question: How is the customer motivated to comply with the writer's request?
Answer: Arousing the interest of a prospective customer and offering to satisfy his or her needs does not, by itself, motivate the customer to buy. The prospective customer has to be helped along the way. A specific offer is a method of converting a general interest into a positive action.

185

A free trial offer for a product that is potentially very useful to a hotel is most attractive. The manager to whom the sample letter is addressed has the option of declining the offer. There is a good chance, however, that he will consider the value of the technological advance, in terms of his organizational efficiency and accept the offer

Key rule 6
Make an offer that the prospective customer cannot refuse.

Question: How is the motivated customer nudged into doing what is wanted?

Answer: In the sales situation it cannot be assumed that a prospective customer does what is best for him or her. A manufacturer believes that if a customer uses the manufacturer's product a benefit is gained. The customer may know that he or she would be better off with the product than without it. Unfortunately, however, this does not mean to say that the product is going to be bought.

Customers need to be pushed or nudged into a buying decision and persuading the customer to make a trial of the product is a good way of doing this.

Key rule 7
Describe the actions that the customer must take.

How many letters?

Question: What factors govern the number of letters that should be written?

Answer: Three major factors dictate how many letters should be written:
1 Typing facilities.
2 Cost.
3 Level of experience of sales personnel.

The decision as to the volume of letters to be sent out is governed by three important factors:

1 *Typing facilities*   There is a limit to the number of prospecting letters that are feasible as part of the normal work load.
2 *Cost*   Additional overhead costs are incurred by the typing facilities required and the preliminary information-seeking calls.
3 *Personnel*   For the inexperienced person, phoning a potential customer after a prospecting letter has been sent is easier than telephoning cold:

> 'Hello Mr Foster. This is Paul Fielding of Canning Distributors Ltd. I wrote to you last week. Did you get my letter?'

In the learning stages of telephone prospecting, any supportive action is of value to the caller.

Certain prospective customer categories are better served by a letter approach than telephoning. A useful plan, in the first three weeks of learning to telephone effectively, is to try out prospecting letters on each of the prospective customer categories in turn.

However, once telephoning skills are acquired, there are no cheaper alternatives.

Summary

Questions	Answers
1 What is the function of the follow-up letter?	The follow-up letter has two functions: 1 To confirm in writing an agreement reached on the telephone. 2 To reopen a discussion or tentative agreement which has taken place on the phone by setting out the salient features.
2 What is the correct way to confirm an order taken on the telephone?	The order confirmation should set out on headed paper all the relevant details of the order instruction. The major details are price, quantity, specification, delivery period, packaging, operating instructions, delivery instructions, payment terms, guarantee and warranty conditions.
3 What is the best formula for writing the prospecting letter?	The formula lies in a set of *Key rules* which apply to all industries and professions: *Key rule 1* Identify the objectives of the prospecting letter. *Key rule 2* Address the customer personally by name, initials, qualifications and title. *Key rule 3* Introduce writer and company. *Key rule 4* Give a reason for writing. *Key rule 5* Offer benefits that satisfy the prospective customer's assessed needs.

Questions	Answers
	Key rule 6
	Make an offer that the prospective customer cannot refuse.
	Key rule 7
	Describe the actions that the customer must take.
4 What factors govern the number of letters that should be written?	Three major factors dictate how many letters should be written:
	1 Typing facilities
	2 Cost
	3 Level of experience of sales personnel

Chapter 12

How to make use of telex, fax and data transmission

Before reading the chapter answer the questions first. Testing your knowledge identifies areas that may need particular attention. The answers are summarised at the end of the chapter.

Questions	Answers

1 What different methods of data transmission are helpful to the sales manager?
2 When seeking new business, what advantage has the telex message over the prospecting phone call?
3 Is there an advantage to the sales manager, in using fax instead of telex to find new business?
4 What guidelines exist for prospecting by telex?
5 In terms of comparative cost for a prospecting campaign, which of the following: phone, letter, telex or fax is the most expensive?

Chapter 12 How to make use of telex, fax and data transmission

Options – The advantages of telex – The benefits of fax – How to send telex messages – Deciding on the right campaign – Summary

Options

Question: What different methods of data transmission are helpful to the sales manager?

Answer: There are three modes of data transmission:
1 Telex
2 Fax
3 High speed data transmission

1 Telex.

Telex is a written text message that is sent very quickly to almost any part of the world. It is typed into a machine terminal, and is received, in a matter of seconds at the destination terminal.

Telex is appropriate for prospecting messages, orders, quotations, instructions, or similar text messages. These can be typed in at any time of the day or night. The message demands an immediate answer. So there can be a 'conversation' between telex users. In the fifty years since telex has been established it has become very sophisticated. For example, it is possible to type in a single call that is sent to one thousand pre-recorded addresses. The telex system is very easy to use. There are three levels of telex user:

(a) The company with a high volume traffic of telex messages, installs the telex machine terminal at its premises.

(b) A computer terminal in the company links through the telephone network, with a telex bureau. A modem is used to make the connection. A telex message can then still be sent at any time of the night or day.

(c) A telex bureau with its own machine terminal sends and receives telex messages for casual users. A small fee is charged for each message sent or received.

2   Fax.

Fax, is the popular word for facsimile. It is a method of sending documents, such as text, pictures, or graphical designs from one point to another. British Telecom liken their fax terminals to photocopiers, linked to each other by domestic telephone lines.

Technically, fax machines scan the documents that are to be sent. They convert what is seen into electrical signals. These signals are sent along a telephone line to the receiving terminal. An exact copy of the original is then reproduced. Anything that can be typed, drawn, written or painted can be sent. Fax is therefore particularly suitable for transmitting technical drawings and numerical data.

Fax is easy to use. There is no need for specialist operator training. Anyone able to use a photocopying machine and a telephone, can use fax. It is also fast. Most machines send an A4 page in less than one minute. With the fastest machines it is about 20 seconds.

There is a wide range of fax machines available on the market. They range from small portable models to those that are very sophisticated. There are two international standards in respect of machines that make use of the telephone network. They are known as Group 2 and Group 3. All machines must be compatible with these standards. The differences between the two groups is cost and speed of transmission. Group 3 transmits a page in less than one minute. Group 2 takes three minutes.

British Telecom publishes a directory of UK Fax users. There are similar directories for the fax users in other countries of the world.

3   High speed data transmission.

Networks of communication centres in key locations

throughout the world, provide a sophisticated range of data transmission services. The significant difference between the sending of telex and fax messages and high speed data transmission is the very high speed at which messages by the latter are sent. Because of this speed, more messages can be sent per minute. Rental costs for the use of a telephone line are the same, whether one message, or fifty are sent per unit of time. High speed data transmission services are therefore able to achieve substantial cost savings. Users of the services are companies such as banks, issuing houses, and multi-national corporations sending a high volume traffic of text messages across the world.

There are various ways through which client users of the communication networks gain access to send their messages. They are – telex machine, word processing terminal, message switcher, mainframe or micro-computer. Depending on the destination, cost savings are quoted as being substantially in excess of 20% over telex message cost.

The advantages of telex

Question: When seeking new business what advantage has the telex message over the prospecting phone call?

Answer: An advantage of telex is the high degree of certainty that telex messages are read by the intended recipient. The prospecting phone call can be successful only when contact is achieved.

In the hands of the skilled person, the phone call is the most cost effective of all methods of prospecting for business. But contact with some well guarded potential customers, may never be achieved. With a skilled person the number is small. When a salesman embarks on a campaign to canvass business by phone, the number of failed contacts is larger.

Without doubt, telex messages and letters are read by the intended recipient. Letters, however, do not have the impact and urgency of the telex message. Unsolicited letters which arrive in the post are often dealt with in a routine fashion.

Telex messages are only received when a company has taken direct steps to send and receive telex messages. Either a telex machine has been purchased or leased, and is installed on the company premises, or a direct link has been established with a telex bureau. Telex messages cost more than letters through the post but by established tradition throughout the world, telex messages are read promptly.

Because the sales manager knows that the telex is going to be read, there are three options:

1 The prime objective of a sale is sought.

We are an old established trading company. From frustrated export order we offer, subject unsold, 10,000 new 2kw Pleasure brand domestic electric heaters 240v, packed ten units per outer carton. Price is £2 per heater. Goods available from Thames Wharf House, 17 Riverside London EC1. Please telex requirements.

2 The telex message is used as a hinge to prepare the addressee to receive a phone call.

Dramatic savings in de-sludging costs have been achieved with our new chemical additive. Exhaustive trials demonstrate 36% cost saving with 25% increased efficiency. Jeffery Barling is phoning Monday 30th between 10.00 am and 10.30 am with full details.

3 The telex message is used to set up an appointment.

Dramatic savings in de-sludging costs have been achieved with our new chemical additive. Exhaustive trials demonstrate 36% cost saving with 25% increased efficiency. Jeffery Barling is in Norwich Monday 30th with samples. Please telex convenient time to call and offer demonstration.

Telex messages offer a positive tool to the sales manager in achieving new business. But that is not to say that they should be used to the exclusion of the phone call, letter or cold canvass. The constraint is cost. Prospecting by telex has limited but powerful functions. There are two principal situations when the use of telex is appropriate.

(a) When the protecting defences of a prospective customer prevent contact with the buyer being made.

(b) As part of an aggressive marketing campaign where resources are available to achieve specific objectives within a set period, e.g. to open twenty new accounts in North West England within a period of six months.

The benefits of fax

Question: Is there an advantage to the sales manager, in using fax instead of telex to find new business?

Answer: Because the fax message can communicate graphic pictures and complex numerical data, in certain circumstances, fax is more effectively persuasive in generating new business.

The first international transmission of fax took place as long ago as the turn of the century. In 1901 a picture of the Pope was sent from London to Paris. But in terms of commercial application, telex has a substantial lead. Telex is very widely used nationally and internationally.

The real growth in fax has taken place in Japan. The Japanese alphabet has some 4000 characters. Fax overcomes the difficulties posed by an alphabet of so many characters for electronic or mechanical text communication. The use of fax in the United Kingdom and elsewhere is growing rapidly in the present time. Within ten to fifteen years, fax may catch up and overtake telex. Meantime, both systems operate.

Telex users have their names and telex numbers in a telex directory which is published by British Telecom. A Call-back Number Directory is also published by British Telecom. The telex message always gives the call-back number:

e.g. 6345112   TUG B G

If an unsolicited telex message is received, and the text does not give details of the sender, the identity of the sender is found in the Call-back Directory.

Fax users, too, have their names in a fax directory. The initial step when prospecting by telex and fax, is the same as when prospecting by phone. A list of names and the numbers of potential customers must be collected.

It has been established that in certain industries the prospecting phone call cannot generate an initial order. It is essential to set up an appointment to make a face-to-face presentation. The same situation applies to the prospecting telex message. With fax, it is different. The increased facility to offer picture reproduction, architectural drawings and designs, or numerical details makes a great difference. Through fax, opportunities to achieve a first contact sale, are now open to art dealers, estate agents, insurance brokers, car dealers, jewellery manufacturers and many other industries. They do not exist when contact is made by telex or phone.

How to send telex messages

Question: What guidelines exist for prospecting by telex?
Answer: There are rules for prospecting by telex in the same way as there are rules for prospecting by phone and letter.

The approach to searching for business by telex must be structured. There is a cost to the telex message that is greater than the cost of the prospecting letter. In the interests of economy, a persuasive literary style must be subordinated to a strictly commercial and businesslike prose style. Unnecessary words and repetition for the sake of dramatic effect, must be avoided.

Golden rule 1
Construct a telex message that is precise, unambiguous and factual.

The message is for a specific person. If it is addressed to 'The Buyer' or 'The Purchasing Officer' the impact is lost. The name of the addressee must be obtained, whether it is available from a directory, or as a result of a phone call to the company itself.

Golden rule 2
Address the message to a specific person by name.

Telex users with their own telex machine installed in-house, may receive many telex messages during the day. The messages themselves are not differentiated, as are letters, by individual notepaper styles and colours. All telex messages are typed out by the telex machine printer on uniform white paper using a standardised print script. It is therefore important that the telex message makes the subject of the message perfectly clear to the reader. Clarity is achieved by a preliminary reference to the subject of the message. This is either in the format of a reference line, e.g.

Ref: Bleep Bleep Paging Unit

or incorporated in the initial wording of the text message, e.g.
Announcing the launch of Bleep Bleep button hole sized transmit/receive paging unit.

Golden rule 3
Introduce the subject of the message at the beginning of the text.

The telex message, by its very nature, reflects a mild state of emergency. Immediate action is appropriate. Otherwise a letter not a telex message would have been sent. To derive full benefit from sending a prospecting telex message, the recipient can be helped into the action that it is desired should happen. The message should state clearly the action to be taken.

Golden rule 4
Complete the text with a clear statement of action to be taken

Example of telex message text

Page 184 illustrates a prospecting letter sent by Puresound Radio Company Ltd to Mr. Ronnie Packard, General Manager, Bedroom Hotel, High Street, Redhill.

Making use of the Golden rules for telex messages, the following text is appropriate when sent in the format of a prospecting telex message:

295441   BUSY   B G
337444   GA 4   G

24.2.85

FOR MR. RONNIE PACKARD
FROM PURESOUND RADIO COMPANY

ANNOUNCING THE LAUNCH OF BLEEP BLEEP BUTTON HOLE SIZED TRANSMIT/RECEIVE PAGING UNIT. THE REVOLUTIONARY MINIATURISED SYSTEM PIONEERS NEW FRONTIERS OF TECHNOLOGY. A FREE 7 DAY TRIAL INSTALLATION IS NOW AVAILABLE FROM YOUR LOCAL DISTRIBUTOR. PLEASE CALL, WITHOUT OBLIGATION, FOR THE DETAILS OF INCREDIBLE USER BENEFIT.

REGARDS
IAN PUSHAR

Deciding on the right campaign

Question: In terms of comparative cost for a prospecting campaign, which of phone, letter, telex or fax is the most expensive?

Answer: A direct comparison of prospecting campaign costs in simple arithmetical terms is not appropriate. The projected success rates of the campaigns with their financial returns are interwoven.

Precise costs of equipment use, per prospecting call, are difficult to determine because there are many variables. The capital costs of telex and fax equipment vary depending on the sophistication and age of the equipment and whether the equipment is leased.

The costs of telex equipment starts from £1300. A dedicated telephone line is required, rental costs of which are approximately £350 per year. Charges at public telephone line rates, are made for the units of time that the line is used. The telex message example above, takes about one minute to transmit.

The cost of fast (Group 3), up-to-date fax machines, is around £3,000. Rental of an ordinary telephone line is approximately £80 per year. Fax is much faster than telex. A high speed fax machine transmits an A4 page in about twenty seconds – compared to several minutes for telex. Although operator handling is pertinent to both telex and fax machines, telex equipment requires that the text is keyed in. Fax machines are able to accommodate

198

original documents. The time of operator involvement for telex is therefore much longer.

With prospecting by telephone, the variable costs are the telephone line rental costs and charges. Cost contributions in respect of the salary of the person making the call are ignored, because they have not been considered in respect of telex and fax.

Prospecting for business by telex or fax is not restricted to those owning or renting the appropriate equipment. A campaign can be conducted through a telex bureau. The bureau used by the author have quoted the following costs:

(a) The time to transmit the above telex message slightly exceeds one minute, but is considered as one minute. The cost of transmitting a one-off telex message of one minute, to anywhere in the United Kingdom, is 90p plus VAT. For 100 telex messages there is a discount of 25%.

(b) The charge for sending one A4 size document by Fax to anywhere in the United Kingdom is £1.50 plus VAT. For 100 fax documents a discount of 25% is applicable.

Details are also provided for the secretarial costs of mounting a prospecting letter campaign. The model letter is that featured on page 184.

Typing the letter, making 100 photocopies, typing names and addresses onto 100 letters and envelopes, folding, inserting, sealing, stamping and posting costs £20 plus VAT. Additionally, there are charges for the postage stamps and the envelopes.

Details of bureaux, high speed data transmission companies and equipment suppliers are provided in Appendix B.

It is important to remember that the telephone, the letter, telex and fax are marketing tools, available to help find new business. They have specialised application. Telephone prospecting is extremely cost effective in the hands of the person who has acquired the appropriate skill. Learning how to sell on the phone, from the pages of this book, takes time and application. The learning process is an additional cost. But the immediate costs of prospecting by telex and fax – higher than straightforward telephone selling – lead to additional benefits.

Summary

Questions

1 What different methods of data transmission are helpful to the sales manager?

2 When seeking new business, what advantage has the telex message over the prospecting phone call?

3 Is there an advantage to the sales manager, in using fax instead of telex to find new business?

4 What guidelines exist for prospecting by telex?

5 In terms of comparative cost for a prospecting campaign, which of phone, letter, telex or fax is the most expensive?

Answers

There are three modes of data transmission:
1 Telex
2 Fax
3 High speed data transmission.

An advantage of telex is the high degree of certainty that the telex messages are read by the intended recipient. The prospecting phone call can be successful only when contact is made.

Because the fax message can communicate graphic pictures and complex numerical data, in certain circumstances, fax is more effectively persuasive in generating new business.

There are rules for prospecting by telex in the same way as there are rules for prospecting by phone and letter.

A direct comparison of prospecting campaign costs in simple arithmetical terms is not appropriate. The projected success rates of the campaigns with their financial returns are interwoven.

Self-help test

This is a DIY test – questions are asked – no answers are provided. The answers must come from you. It is only by mastering the techniques covered in this book that you really will win *more* business by phone.

Questions   ## Answers

1 Do I understand that real
  skill on the telephone leads
  to more business and more
  profit?
2 Do I want to be a person
  who uses the telephone
  very effectively?
3 Am I going to make the
  effort?
4 When?
5 How am I going to
  start?
6 Am I scared?
7 What happens if it doesn't
  work?
8 How do I prospect for
  business?
9 What essential records do I
  keep?
10 What success rate do I aim
   for?
11 How do I improve my
   success rate?

Questions   ## Answers

12   What is the most effective
     way to make appoint-
     ments?

13   How do I deal with gate-
     keepers?

14   What is the best way to get
     past secretaries?

15   What do I do when the
     buyer is out?

16   How do I introduce myself?

17   What is to be done when
     the buyer says 'No'?

18   How are customer needs
     qualified?

19   What is a benefit message?

20   What is the way to give a
     benefit message?

21   What is the function of a
     trial close?

22   What do I do when I am not
     getting sales?

23   Why do customers raise
     objections?

24   How do I overcome the
     customer objections?

25   What happens when cus-
     tomers argue?

26   What technique can I use to
     stop getting angry on the
     phone?

27   How do I communicate
     most effectively?

28   When do customers mean
     what they say?

29   What is the best way of
     dealing with customers'
     questions?

30   How do I turn a quotation
     into an order?

Questions	Answers
31 What is the best way to save a cancelled order?	
32 What is the best way to get repeat business?	
33 How do I plan my personal time most effectively?	
34 What is the best way to plan the sales presentation?	
35 How long should the sales presentation last?	
36 How does a buyer think?	
37 What are the main types of sales presentation?	
38 What makes buyers buy?	
39 What are buying signals?	
40 What is the best way to close?	
41 What obstacles to closing are met?	
42 What should be done if the close is not successful?	
43 What is the best way to get repeat business?	
44 How do I make customers satisfied?	
45 What is the best way to handle complaints?	
46 What is the real value of the follow-up call?	
47 What is the telephone caller's Achilles' heel?	
48 Why are orders lost on the telephone?	
49 What are the rules for answering the telephone?	
50 What has telephoning to do with PR?	
51 What is the function of the follow-up letter?	

Questions

52 What is the correct way to confirm an order taken on the telephone?

53 How do I write a prospecting letter?

54 How many prospecting letters should I write?

Answers

Appendix A

Useful names of directories and sources

Professional

The Medical Directory
Churchill Livingstone, Publishers, 5 Bentinck Street, London W1
(01 935 0121)

Institute of Chartered Accountants in England, Wales and Scotland
PO Box 433, Chartered Accountants Hall, Moorgate Place, London EC2P 2BJ
(01 628 7060)

Annual Register of Pharmaceutical Chemists
Pharmaceutical Society of Great Britain, 1 Lambeth High Street, London SE1 7JN
(01 735 9141)

Opticians Register
General Optical Council, 41 Harley Street, London W1N 2DJ
(01 580 3898)

Register of Architects
Architects Registration Council of UK, 73 Hallam Street, London W1N 6EJ
(01 580 5861)

Solicitors Diary and Directory
Waterlow Publications Ltd, Maxwell House, 74 Worship Street, London
EC2A 2EN
(01 377 4719)

Royal Institute of Chartered Surveyors
12 Great George Street, Parliament Square, London SW1P 3AZ
(01 222 7000)

Kemps Estate Agents Yearbook and Directory
Kemps Group (Printers and Publishers) Ltd, 1–5 Bath Street, London EC1V 9QA
(01 253 4761)

Industrial

Kompass
Kompass Publishers Ltd, Windsor Court, East Grinstead House, East Grinstead,
West Sussex RH19 1XD
(0342 26972)

The Times 1000
Times Books Ltd, 16 Golden Square, London W1R 4BN
(01 434 3767)

Commercial

The British Clothing Industry Year Book
Kemps Publishing Group, 1–5 Bath Street, London EC1V 9QA
(01 253 4761)

International Film and Year Book
Kemps Publishing Group, 1–5 Bath Street, London EC1V 9QA
(01 253 4761)

Music and Recording Industry Year Book
Kemps Publishing Group, 1–5 Bath Street, London EC1V 9QA
(01 253 4761)

Computer Users' Year Book
CUYB Publishing Ltd, 430–2 Holdenhurst Road, Bournemouth BH8 9AA
(0202 302464)

Printers' Yearbook
British Printing Industry Federation, 11 Bedford Row, London WC1R 4DX
(01 242 6904)

Electrical and Electronics Trades Directory
Peter Peregrinus Ltd, Marketing Department, Station House, Nightingale Road, Hitchin, Herts SC5 1RJ
(0462 53331)

Bankers Almanac and Year Book
Thomas Skinner Directories, Windsor Court, East Grinstead House, East Grinstead, West Sussex RH19 1XD
(0342 26972)

National Register of Housebuilders and Developers
National House Building Council, 58 Portland Place, London W1N 4BU
(01 637 1248)

British Club Year Book and Directory
Joelmead Ltd, 63b Lansdowne Place, Hove, Sussex BN3 1F4
(0273 773174)

Business Equipment Guide
BED Books Ltd, 44 Wallington Square, Wallington, Surrey SM6 8RG
(01 647 1001)

Retail

Yellow Pages
Post Office Yellow Pages, 10–18 Manor Gardens, London N7 6JY
(Directories suppled by British Telecom – telephone area offices)

Kellys Directories
Kellys Directories Ltd, Windsor Court, East Grinstead House, East Grinstead, West Sussex RH19 1XD
(0342 26972)

The Antique Shops of Great Britain
Antique Collectors Club Ltd, 5 Church Street, Woodbridge, Suffolk
(03943 5501)

Retail Directory
Newman Books Ltd, 48 Poland Street, London W1V 4PP
(01 439 0355)

Public sector

Recreation Management Handbook
E. & F. Spon Ltd, 11 New Fetter Lane, London EC4P 4EE
(01 583 9855)

Hospitals and Health Services Year Book
Institute of Health Service Administrators, 75 Portland Place, London W1N 4AN
(01 580 5041)

Charities Digest
Family Welfare Association, 501–5 Kingsland Road, Dalston, London E8 4AD
(01 254 6251)

Local Authority Electoral Rolls
(available at town halls and public libraries)

Councils, Committees and Boards
CBD Research Ltd, 154 High Street, Beckenham, Kent
(01 650 7745)

Current British Directories
CBD Research Ltd, 154 High Street, Beckenham, Kent
(01 650 7745)

British Rate and Data (BRAD)
76 Oxford Street, London W1N 0HH
(01 637 7511)

Who Owns Who
Dun and Bradstreet Ltd, Publications Division, 6–8 Bonhill Street, London EC2A 4BU
(01 628 3691)

Association of British Directory Publishers Imperial House, 17 Kingsway, London WC2B 6UN
(01 386 7111)

Arab Marketing Directory
Benns Hardware Directory
Benns Press Directory

Binding Data Index
Building Board Directory
Chemical Industries Directory
Chemists and Druggists Directory
Contract Carpeting
Directory to the Furnishing Trade
Export Data
Fire Protection Data
Forestry and British Timber Directory
Gas Directory and Who's Who
Gifts Annual Buyers Guide
International Shipping and Shipbuilding Directory
Leather Guide
Offset Data Index
Phillips Paper Trade Directory
Printing Trade Directory
Sports Trades Annual Buyers Guide
Timber Trade Directory
Woodworking Industry Buyers Guide

All available from: Benn Publications Ltd, Sovereign Way, Tonbridge, Kent TN9 1RW
(0732 364422)

209

Appendix B

Useful sources of telex, fax and data transmission

Telex/fax Bureau

Telex Business Services, 291 Cricklewood Lane, London NW2
(01 445 9962)

High speed data transmission company

Vitel International Ltd, Vitel House, Albert Road, London NW4
(01 203 6655)

Telex, fax and data transmission equipment and service

BTI Business Box, Garrard House, 7th floor, 31–45 Gresham Street,
London EC2V 7DN
(01 936 2922)

Index